ELECTRICAL LICENSING EXAM
POWER PRACTICE

LEARNINGEXPRESS®

NEW YORK

Cataloging-in-Publication Data is on file with the Library of Congress.

ISBN 978-1-61103-093-8

Printed in the United States of America

9 8 7 6 5 4 3 2

For more information on LearningExpress, other LearningExpress products, or bulk sales, please write to us at:
  224 W. 29th Street
  3rd Floor
  New York, NY 10001

CONTENTS ▶

ABOUT THE AUTHOR

Tracey Arvin is the Department Chair and Professor in the Electrical Technology programs at the Benjamin Franklin Institute of Technology in Boston, MA. Ms. Arvin is a Licensed Vocational Educator in the state of Massachusetts with over 15 years of classroom experience. Ms. Arvin holds both a Journeyman's and Master's Electrician License and has over 25 years of industry experience which includes industrial installations and control systems, commercial and residential construction, and small business ownership. She has a Bachelor's of Arts Liberal Studies, with a concentration in Vocational Education, from Framingham State College; a Bachelor's of Science in Geology and Earth Science from Salem State College; and a Master's of Science in Geology and Geophysics, from Boston College.

1 ▶ ALL ABOUT THE NEC AND YOUR LICENSING EXAM

Whether you are just starting out in the electrical trade or are a seasoned veteran looking for career enhancement, successful completion of the *Electrical Licensing Exam Power Practice* is an important step in your career.

The electrical industry is an exciting and dynamic field that employs skilled tradespeople across the country. Electricians perform a variety of tasks in many different areas including residential, commercial, and industrial electrical installations. Workers entering this field must be well trained for the task at hand or injuries and loss of property may occur. For that reason, most states and municipalities require electrical licensure and/or certification for those who are installing electrical systems and maintaining equipment. Governing bodies within individual states mandate the requirements for licensure and certification to perform electrical work for hire.

Each state may have multiple levels of licensure/certification available, with each providing various entitled duties and/or responsibilities. These certifications may include but are not limited to: Systems Technician, Electrical Contractor, Journeyman Electrician, and Master Electrician. The most common qualification is the Journeyman Electrician license. We have focused this book specifically on certification for a Journeyman Electrician license.

Requirements for Journeyman Electrician Licensure

Although the requirements for Journeyman Electrician Licensure may vary, typically they include three fundamental aspects:

- **Apprentice Work Experience:** on-the-job training under the direct supervision of a licensed electrician. Time in this phase varies by state; a typical requirement is 8,000 hours (four years) of legally obtained practical experience in wiring for, installing, and repairing of electrical apparatus and equipment for light, heat, and power. This phase of the process is known as an apprenticeship.
- **Education:** formal classroom educational hours focusing on the requirements of the **National Electric Code** and electrical theory.
- **Examination:** passing an examination that tests the knowledge of the **National Electric Code** and electrical theory (this book focuses on this aspect of the process).

NFPA 70— The National Electric Code

The National Electric Code (NEC) is a living document in that it is reviewed and revised continually as technology changes and hazard abatement is recognized. Its purpose is the "practical safeguarding of people and property from hazards arising from the use of electricity" (**Section 90.1**). Every three years, volunteers from across the country and the industry participate in the process of submitting, reviewing, and implementing proposals for change. This process is overseen by the National Fire Protection Association (NFPA), a nonprofit organization devoted to eliminating death, injury, property, and economic loss due to fire, as well as electrical and related hazards. The **NEC** is just one of hundreds of codes and standards that the NFPA publishes pertaining to life safety.

While the continual revising of the NEC provides safer installations of electrical systems, it can cause additional confusion on the part of users of the code. An understanding of the format and organization of the code will help to eliminate confusion and allow you to quickly obtain information.

Organization of the NEC

If you look to the Table of Contents of the NEC and at Figure 1, you will find there are 12 separate areas outlined: Article 90 Introduction, Chapters 1–8, Chapter 9 Tables, Annexes, and Index. The introduction and chapters 1–8 are the enforceable rules of the code.

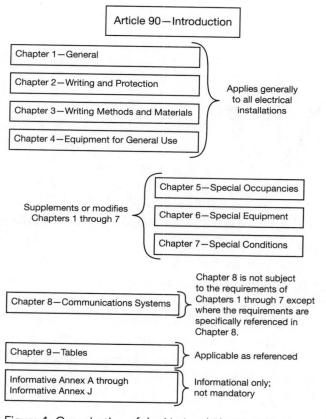

Figure 1: Organization of the National Electrical Code

Reprinted with permission from NFPA 70® 2017. *National Electrical Code*®, Copyright 2016, National Fire Protection Association, Quincy, MA. This reprinted material is not the complete and official position of the NFPA on the referenced subject, which is represented only by the standard in its entirety.

Article 90 Introduction

This section will provide you with many details necessary for you to navigate the code. The purpose of the code is found in **Section 90.1** and is stated previously. Included in other sections are administrative provisions including, scope, arrangement, enforcement, and formal interpretation of the document.

Section 90.5

This section explains the language of the code that is essential to adherence to the rules and how they may be used. Specifically, *Mandatory Rules* are actions that are required or prohibited and are characterized by *shall* or *shall not*. (See Figure 2.) *Permissive Rules* are actions that are allowed but not required and characterized by *"shall be permitted"* and *"shall not be required."* (See Figure 3.)

VII. Service Equipment—Overcurrent Protection

230.90 Where Required. Each ungrounded service conductor shall have overload protection.

(A) Ungrounded Conductor. Such protection <u>shall be</u> provided by an overcurrent device in series with each ungrounded service conductor that has a rating or setting not higher than the allowable ampacity of the conductor. A set of fuses <u>shall be</u> considered all the fuses required to protect all the ungrounded conductors of a circuit. Single-pole circuit breakers, grouped in accodance with 230.71(B), shall be considered as one protective device.

Figure 2: Section 230.90(A) Example of a *Mandatory Rule*

230.82 Equipment Connected to the Supply Side of Service Disconnect. Only the following equipment <u>shall be permitted</u> to be connected to the supply side of the service disconnecting means:

Figure 3: Section 230.82 Example of a *Permissive Rule*

Reprinted with permission from NFPA 70® 2017. *National Electrical Code*®, Copyright 2016, National Fire Protection Association, Quincy, MA. This reprinted material is not the complete and official position of the NFPA on the referenced subject, which is represented only by the standard in its entirety.

Chapters 1–8, the Body of the NEC

These are the major subdivisions, and enforceable rules of the **NEC**. Each chapter has been carefully crafted to include rules specific to broad areas of the wiring of electrical systems.

Chapters 1–4 apply generally to all electrical installations:

- **Chapter 1—General**
- **Chapter 2—Wiring and Protection**
- **Chapter 3—Wiring Methods and Materials**
- **Chapter 4—Equipment for General Use**

Chapters 5–7 supplements or modifies Chapters 1–7:

- **Chapter 5—Special Occupancies**
- **Chapter 6—Special Equipment**
- **Chapter 7—Special Conditions**

Chapter 8 Communications Systems: These stand alone; no other rules within the previous chapters apply unless specially stated as such.

Each chapter of the NEC contains rules specific to a particular area of electrical installations. As each chapter may contain a vast number of rules, each is subdivided to allow you to quickly locate the information that you need to perform your work.

KEY POINT

Keep in mind that the rules are prescriptive—there is generally no formal explanation contained in the **NEC**. The second sentence of **Art. 90.1(A) Purpose** states "This *Code* is not intended as a design specification or an instruction manual for untrained persons."

Subdivisions of Chapters

- **Articles:** subdivisions of chapters covering specific subjects such as **Article 240 Overcurrent Protection** and **Article 310 Conductors for General Wiring**. Articles are further divided into sections and occasionally parts. Note that the first number of an article corresponds to the chapter in which it is contained (**Article 100** is located in Chapter 1).

- **Parts:** especially large articles may be organized further into parts, a logical grouping of similar information. For example, Article 250 Grounding and Bonding, is divided into 10 separate parts. Note that parts are designated by Roman numerals (see Figure 4).

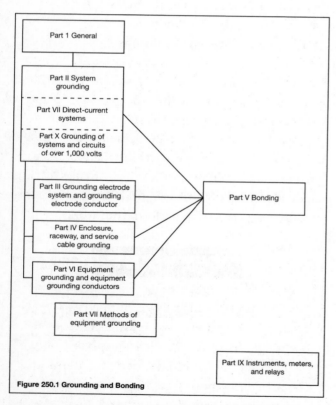

Figure 250.1 Grounding and Bonding

Figure 4: Parts of Article 250 Grounding and Bonding

- **Sections:** contain specific and individual rules within an article. These are designated by the numbers that follow the decimal point. For example, **430.52** indicates **Section 52** of **Article 430 Motors**. For ease of use and clarity, sections may be subdivided further into *subsections*.

- **Subsections:** may be divided into up to three levels and are designated as follows (see Figure 5):
  - Level 1 – Capital letters within parenthesis
  - Level 2 – Numbers within parenthesis
  - Level 3 – Lower case letters within parenthesis

- **Exceptions:** some rules contain exceptions that may be utilized when absolutely necessary. Exceptions immediately follow the specific rule that they apply to and are always italicized (see Figure 5). They may also be numbered if more than one applies to a specific rule.

- **Informational Notes:** are not an enforceable part of the **NEC**. They are included to provide explanations of the material, examples, design suggestions, and references to other areas of the NEC or other codes and standards (see Figure 5).

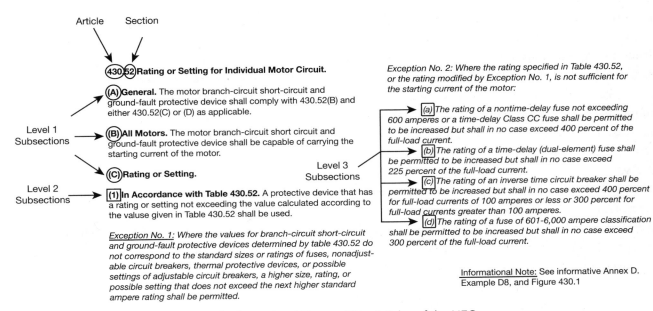

Figure 5: Subdivisions, Exceptions, and Informational Notes within Articles of the NEC

Reprinted with permission from NFPA 70® 2017. *National Electrical Code®*, Copyright 2016, National Fire Protection Association, Quincy, MA. This reprinted material is not the complete and official position of the NFPA on the referenced subject, which is represented only by the standard in its entirety.

KEY POINT

One important note to new users of the code is that the chapters and articles are written in a *tiered format*, in which a rule only applies to the subsection, section, and article where it resides. Inexperienced code users will often try to apply rules from one section to other sections of the code. This will only lead to confusion and misapplications of the NEC.

Chapter 9 Tables

The tables in Chapter 9 contain mandatory requirements of the **NEC** that pertain primarily to conductors, raceways, and the parameters for power limitations for power-limited circuits. However, the information in each table may only be utilized if specifically referenced in Chapters 1–8. For example,

Section 344.22 of **Article 344 Rigid Metal Conduit: Type RMC** is entitled **Number of Conductors**. The first paragraph states that "The number of conductors shall not exceed that permitted by the percentage full specified in Table 1, Chapter 9."

Annexes

There are 10 Informative Annexes indicated by A-J located in the latter portion of the NEC. As clearly stated in Section 90.3 Code Arrangement, and at the beginning of each annex, "*informative annexes are not a part of the requirements of this NFPA document but are included for informational purposes only.*"

If you are a new user of the NEC, you should become familiar with the useful information contained within the annexes such as Annex A Product Standards, Annex E Construction Types, and Annex I Tightening Torque Tables. But particular attention should be paid to **Annex D Examples**, which provide examples for common calculations required by the NEC such as **Example D1(a) One-Family Dwelling** service calculations listed in **Article 220 Branch-Circuit, Feeder, and Service Calculations, Part III Feeder and Service Load Calculations**. There will be several questions on your licensing exam where calculations will be required; these sections can help to prepare you for success.

Index

As with any other book, the Index is found in the back of the NEC and lists alphabetically important words, phrases, equipment, conditions, and locations included throughout the text. You can use the Index as a very powerful tool to quickly locate and access the rules and information you need. While you might be tempted to reference the Table of Contents to locate specific information contained within a book, doing so in the NEC may lead to a chapter or article containing hundreds of rules to wade through. There is simply too much information in the NEC to include more specifics in the Table of Contents.

Revisions of the National Electric Code

The NFPA oversees the process responsible for developing and updating the NEC. This process is full, open, and consensus based, meaning that anyone can participate and that all proposals and comments shall be addressed. The NEC is revised on a 3-year cycle, and as soon as an edition is published, the cycle begins again. The NFPA Standards Counsel appoints Technical Committees and Code Making Panels (CMP), consisting of hundreds of professionals throughout the industry including electrical installers, wiring inspectors, equipment manufacturers, fire protection professionals, Occupational Health and Safety Administration (OSHA) staff, and nationally recognized testing laboratories. All appointees serve on a volunteer basis. The membership and responsibilities of all committees and panels can be found immediately following the Table of Contents in the NEC.

How the Process Works

The public is encouraged to submit proposals, known as inputs, for changes they think should be made to the current edition of the NEC. These inputs go before the CMP responsible for the article for which the change is suggested. The CMP's formally address all suggestions and vote to accept, accept in part, or reject the input. All of their determinations are published in a document referred to as the First Draft. The public is invited to review and submit comments on the First Draft. A time limit is placed on the comment stage; once expired, the CMP's again review and vote on the submitted comments. The result is the publication of the Second Draft. There is one more opportunity for public input; this comes in the form of a Notice of Intent to Make a Motion (NITMAM), which can be submitted by anyone. The committees and panels take a final vote before the issuance of the new standard. The entire process takes approximately 2 years to complete. The First and Second Drafts can be viewed, and inputs and comments may be submitted online at www.nfpa.org.

2017 National Electric Code

This current edition of the NEC was published and made available to the public in November 2016. The public submitted 4012 inputs for change—of those, 1,235 were voted into the First Draft Report, upon which 1,513 public comments were received and an additional 569 changes were voted into the Second Draft Report. Changes that made the final publication of the standard include four new articles and hundreds of revised sections and definitions.

State Adoption of the NEC

Although written and published for the benefit of the entire country, and many other countries around the world, the NEC does not go into effect unless formally adopted by individual states. Just as each state governs its own licensing/certifications of electrical installers, so they must choose to accept the NEC. It is the responsibility of the individual student or installer to utilize the proper edition of the NEC in their state.

The Electrical Licensing Exam

The goal of the exam is two pronged: (1) to test knowledge and (2) to determine whether applicants can apply electrical codes in real-world situations. The electrical licensing exam tests an individual's knowledge of the industry, primarily code and theory, instead of their physical skills and abilities. To do otherwise would be impractical, expensive, and time consuming. The exam covers a wide variety of information used throughout the industry, some of which may not be typically used on a daily basis by average electricians. Instead of assessing an individual's abilities as an electrician, the exam assesses one's ability to find information within the **NEC**. Adequate preparation for the exam in the form of taking practice exams, and repeatedly locating information in the code book, is paramount for you to succeed in passing the licensing exam and fulfilling your dream to become a licensed/certified Journeyman Electrician.

Types of Exams

Exams are computer generated and may contain multiple parts. Most states use PSI, an online testing organization. Details of your individual state examination processes may be found on the PSI website: https://candidate.psiexams.com, or by contacting your state and local governing board. Information is often presented in the form of "Candidate Information Bulletins" and should include the cost of the exam, where it can be taken, what to bring with you, and general content of the exam.

An open book exam format is the most common in use today. Open book means that reference materials are allowed to be used while testing. This is different than a closed book format where you would need to memorize the rules of the NEC in order to pass the exam. While it is an advantage to have reference materials available, keep in mind that most exams have a time limit. Typical time per question is between 2–3 minutes. This makes preparing for the exam and practicing even more important.

The references allowed during your exam will include the state's adopted edition of the National Electric Code book. Code books may be indexed, highlighted, and annotated. Other reference materials could include state adopted amendments to the **NEC**, state laws and regulations pertaining to electrical work for hire, and other NFPA standards such as NFPA 72—National Fire Alarm Code. Please be sure to refer to your applicable Candidate Information Bulletin before arriving to take your exam.

Content

In order for you to be fully prepared for your licensing exam you must know what subjects are covered, what form the questions will be written in, how much time will be available, and what score is required to pass.

A typical exam consists of 80 questions and a time limit of 4 hours, or 240 minutes. This amounts to 3 minutes per question. Content will vary from state to state, but will most likely be similar to that which is represented in Figure 6. Most of the questions are derived from topics that are found within the National Electric Code book. Others, such as electrical theory questions, are covered in other reference books that may or may not be allowed inside the testing facility. Be sure to adequately prepare by referring to your state's requirements.

TOPIC	NUMBER OF QUESTIONS
Electrical Wiring Methods and Electrical Materials	18
Special Occupancies, Equipment, and Conditions	9
Branch Circuit Calculations and Conductors	15
Electrical Equipment and Devices	10
Motors and Generators	5
Electrical Services, Service Equipment, and Separately Derived Systems	9
Definitions, Calculations, Theory, and Plans	6
Electrical Feeders	3
Electrical Control Devices and Disconnecting Means	3
Renewable Energy	2
Total	80

Figure 6. Content and Subjects Covered in Licensing Exam

When and Where to Take the Exam

Once you have fulfilled the requirements of your apprenticeship by completing and documenting your education and work experiences, you are ready to apply to sit for the licensing exam. Documentation, applications, and fees are typically submitted to your state or local governing board. Once these boards have reviewed and approved your application, you will receive a notice of eligibility. It is then your responsibility to contact the testing organization (PSI for example) to schedule your exam. Depending on the size of your state, there may be several testing locations for the convenience of test-takers.

On the day of the exam, you should arrive at least 30 minutes early in order to sign-in and familiarize yourself with the examination process. Most states require at least one form of picture ID. Wear comfortable clothing and dress in layers in order to insure that you experience no physical distractions such as being too hot or too cold. Be sure to bring the allowed reference material and a calculator if acceptable.

How the Exam Is Scored

Your scores will be based on the number of questions you have answered correctly. A passing score is a minimum of 70%. Scoring is achieved automatically for computerized tests. Once the time limit expires, your score will be provided to you immediately. A score report may also be available to you either immediately, or mailed at a later date. This report might indicate your areas of strength and weakness, and may be helpful to guide your future study if you do not pass the first time you take the exam.

How to Use the *Electrical Licensing Exam Power Practice* Book

The best way to succeed in passing the electrical licensing exam the first time is to know how to locate information quickly in the NEC, and *practice, practice, practice*. This book will help you achieve these goals.

There are five practice exams included with this book—four in the physical book and one online, which you can access by going to the final page of this book. Each exam has been prepared to resemble actual licensing exams. The exams consist of 80 multiple-choice questions, which focus on all aspects of the 2017 National Electrical Code and related electrical theory.

Prepare to take the Power Practice Exams in the same way that you would the actual licensing exam;

- Find a quiet comfortable place to work where you will be undisturbed
- Set aside a specific amount of time—we recommend you allow 4 hours per exam or 3 minutes per question
- Gather the same materials that will be allowed on test day including a well-indexed and annotated code book, pencils and erasers (if you are taking one of the 3 paper exams) or a computer with Internet access, and any other reference material that may be allowed on test day

How to Take the Power Practice Exams

When taking a timed, multiple-choice exam:

- Answer questions you feel confident about first. These might include questions that you don't feel the need to use reference materials to find the correct answers, and those which require a simple calculation to solve. The goal is to quickly answer as many questions as possible, leaving plenty of time to look up the more challenging questions in your **NEC** and reference material.
- Next, go back to the questions you were not able to answer off the top of your head. Carefully read the questions and the answers, and eliminate any unreasonable answer choices first. Once you have the answer choices narrowed down, use resources to find the correct answer. Be sure to keep an eye on the time as you won't want to spend an extended amount of time on any single question.

When you have completed each Power Practice Exam:

- Use the answer key to score your exam and determine whether or not you passed.
- Each question has only 1 correct answer.
  - The answer key provides the correct answer and the section of the code where the answer can be found
  - The answer key also contains reasons why the other choices are incorrect
  - Theory answers have the appropriate formula and solution included

What to do if you don't do well on the Power Practice Exams:

- Review every question that was answered incorrectly, making sure to reference the appropriate code section and/or review the formula being used.
- Review ways in which the correct answers could be found. One unique aspect of the NEC is that information may be located in a variety of ways. Use the examples we provide in the answer keys, and explore some of your own. The more familiar you are with your code book, and what strategies work best for you, the more likely you are to succeed with your goal of becoming a licensed electrician.

Now you're ready to move forward with powerful practice. Best of luck with your prep and your certification!

2 ▶ PRACTICE TEST 1

This practice exam was designed to reflect the format, level, specifications, and content found on typical state tests for Journeyman Electrician certification/licensing. It contains questions based on the 2017 National Electrical Code and related electrical theory.

Official Journeyman Electrician examinations are typically open book tests. This means that you will be allowed to bring and reference any bound copy of the *National Electrical Code® 2017 Edition* during testing. You should also feel free to do so for this practice examination, but it is highly recommended that you check with your state's licensing board to confirm your state's specific testing requirements and allowances.

The official tests are typically four hours (240 minutes). If you would like to practice answering questions under test-like conditions, be sure to set a timer and take the exam in a quiet place where you will be undisturbed for the duration.

After you are finished, evaluate how you did with the answers and explanations immediately following the practice test. Your scores will be based on the number of questions you have answered correctly. A passing score is a minimum of 70%, so your goal is to answer a minimum of 56 questions correctly.

Good luck!

1. Cables installed within notches in wood members require protection against nails or screws by using a steel plate at least _____ thick, installed before the building finish is applied. A thinner plate that provides equal or better protection may be used where listed and marked.
   a. $\frac{1}{16}$ in.
   b. $\frac{1}{8}$ in.
   c. $\frac{3}{8}$ in.
   d. $\frac{1}{2}$ in.

2. Where direct-buried conductors and cables emerge from grade, they must be protected by enclosures or raceways to a point _____ above finished grade.
   a. 3 ft.
   b. 6 ft.
   c. 8 ft.
   d. 10 ft.

3. In a mobile home where distribution equipment (either circuit breaker or fuse type) is installed, the bottom of such equipment shall be located a minimum of how far from the floor level of the mobile home?
   a. 12 in.
   b. 24 in.
   c. 36 in.
   d. 48 in.

4. According to NEC 240.4(D)(1), 18 AWG copper conductor overcurrent protection cannot exceed how many amperes?
   a. 2
   b. 5
   c. 7
   d. 10

5. The maximum length for a kitchen waste disposer cord is
   a. 6 in.
   b. 12 in.
   c. 24 in.
   d. 36 in.

6. In the NEC, which table gives assistance in determining the allowable ampacity (ampere capacity) of a THHN conductor installed in raceways, cables, or earth?
   a. 310.15(B)(16)
   b. 402.3
   c. 620.11(C)
   d. 705.12(D)(2)

7. For a portable motor, what is the minimum horsepower rating that the controller can be for an attachment plug and receptacle or cord connector?
   a. $\frac{1}{3}$
   b. $\frac{1}{2}$
   c. 1
   d. $1\frac{1}{2}$

8. The ampacity of capacitor circuit conductors should not be less than what percentage of the capacitor's rated current?
   a. 80
   b. 90
   c. 120
   d. 135

9. When in parallel, conductors must match in all ways EXCEPT
   a. circular mil area
   b. insulation color
   c. conductor material
   d. terminations

10. The maximum operating temperature for RHH thermoset in a dry or damp location is
  a. 32°C
  b. 60°C
  c. 75°F
  d. 194°F

11. Which section permits nonmetallic-sheathed cable branch circuits to be installed temporarily in structures without specific regard for height limitations?
  a. 334.10(3)
  b. 590.4(C)
  c. 830.40(B)
  d. None of the above

12. The definition for the electrical phrase "in sight from" appears in what NEC Article/Section?
  a. 100
  b. 240.6
  c. 312.11
  d. 430.102

13. In electrical terms, which of the following locations would not be subject to the strict requirements typically found in the patient-care space of a healthcare facility?
  a. Examining rooms
  b. Nursing home sleeping rooms
  c. Wet procedure spaces
  d. Treatment rooms

14. A receptacle device that receives two nonmetallic-sheathed cables, 14-2 with ground, will have a total cubic inch box fill count of
  a. 2
  b. 4
  c. 7
  d. 14

15. Electricians shall be permitted to use knob-and-tube wiring only when working
  a. on new installations.
  b. in commonwealths.
  c. on extensions to existing installations.
  d. All of the above

16. NEC Table _____ lists the minimum sizes of equipment grounding conductors for grounding raceways and equipment.
  a. 250.102(C)(1)
  b. 250.122
  c. 250.66
  d. 310.15(B)(16)

17. Determine the applied voltage to the circuit below. The total resistance equals 20 Ω, and the total current through the circuit equals 6 amperes.

  a. 120 volts
  b. 12 volts
  c. 3.33 volts
  d. 0.3 volts

18. When seven elevators are installed on one feeder, the demand factor permitted is
  a. 0.77
  b. 0.88
  c. 0.92
  d. 1.00

19. A load that receives power for at least three hours at a time is considered _____.
a. contiguous
b. half-day
c. continuous
d. triple

20. A ground ring shall be installed _____ below the surface of the Earth.
a. 8 in.
b. 12 in.
c. 30 in.
d. 36 in.

21. The motors, controllers, and wiring of electrically operated pool covers shall be located no less than _____ from the inside wall of the pool unless they are separated from the pool by a wall, a cover, or another permanent barrier.
a. 1 ft.
b. 2 ft.
c. 4 ft.
d. 5 ft.

22. The minimum circuit ampacity to supply the required GFCI bathroom(s) receptacle outlet(s) is _____.
a. 15 amps
b. 20 amps
c. 25 amps
d. 30 amps

23. Aluminum grounding electrode conductors shall not be terminated within _____ from the Earth.
a. 4 inches
b. 12 inches
c. 18 inches
d. 36 inches

24. Which of the following NEC sections covers ungrounded systems?
a. 110.14(C)
b. 250.4(B)
c. 501.15(A)
d. 668.11(C)

25. The symbol you would find on a plan or diagram to indicate a switch that can control a load from two different locations is _____.
a. S
b. S_2
c. S_3
d. S_4

26. According to NEC Section(s) _____, electricians shall not exceed 75% of an area when splicing and taping conductors in surface metal raceways.
a. 312.8(2)
b. 386.56
c. 398.3
d. 312.8(2) and 386.56

27. For determining farm load demand factors, use NEC Table
a. 210.24
b. 220.103
c. C.11(A)
d. None of the above

28. In a Class ____, Division _____ location, combustible dust may, in abnormal operations, be in quantities sufficient to produce explosive or ignitable mixtures.
   a. I
   b. II
   c. III
   d. IV

   a. I
   b. II
   c. III
   d. IV

29. Electricians who are running isolated receptacles to reduce electronic noise (EMF) should consider NEC Section _____.
   a. 250.122
   b. 250.146(D)
   c. 406.10(E)
   d. 645.15

30. Which of the following NEC Articles establishes the requirements for fixed electric space-heating equipment?
   a. 210
   b. 422
   c. 424
   d. 427

31. In commercial and industrial service and feeder calculations, a receptacle outlet shall be calculated at _____ volt-amperes for each single or multiple receptacle on one yoke.
   a. 120
   b. 180
   c. 240
   d. 360

32. Direct burial cable extending from a one- and two-family residential dwelling to a post light not protected by a GFCI must be buried at least _____ in the Earth to the finished grade.
   a. 18 in.
   b. 24 in.
   c. 3 ft.
   d. 4 ft.

33. Each unit length of heating cable shall be marked with all of the following except _____.
   a. identifying name or identification symbol
   b. catalog number
   c. rating in volts and watts or volts and amperes
   d. insulation temperature limitations

34. NEC Article _____, Part ____ governs cartridge fuses.
   a. 240
   b. 300
   c. 430
   d. 500

   a. II
   b. III
   c. IV
   d. VI

35. The requirements for audio signal-processing equipment are outlined in which NEC chapter?
   a. 5
   b. 6
   c. 7
   d. None of above

36. Which of the following insulated conductor types is permitted in dry and damp locations?
   a. PFA
   b. THHW
   c. FEP
   d. All of the above

37. For kitchen countertops and work surface wall space, the minimum width that requires a receptacle outlet is _____.
  a. 8 in.
  b. 12 in.
  c. 14 in.
  d. 18 in.

38. Unless otherwise provided, type AC cable shall be secured within _____ in. of every outlet box, junction box, cabinet, or fitting and at intervals not exceeding _____ ft. where installed on or across framing members.
  a. 8
  b. 12
  c. 16
  d. 18

  a. 3
  b. 4.5
  c. 6
  d. 8

39. In a dwelling, receptacles shall be installed such that no point measured horizontally along the floor line of any wall space is more than _____ feet from a receptacle outlet.
  a. 2
  b. 4
  c. 6
  d. 12

40. When used as listed in patient bed locations of critical care areas, the grounding terminal of a hospital-grade receptacle must connect to ground by which of the following?
  a. Bare equipment grounding conductor
  b. Wire one gauge larger than that used for the other conductors
  c. Insulated copper equipment grounding conductor
  d. Any of the above

41. Which of the following locations within a dwelling unit requires AFCI protection on all 120-volt, single-phase, 15- and 20-ampere branch circuits?
  a. Laundry areas
  b. Bedrooms
  c. Kitchen
  d. All of the above

42. Overhead branch circuit conductors that are outdoors must be protected with coverings and/or insulated for a minimum distance of _____ feet beyond the building.
  a. 5
  b. 6
  c. 10
  d. 25

43. Outside branch circuit and feeder open conductors shall be separated from open conductors of other circuits or systems by not less than _____.
  a. 50 mm
  b. 200 mm
  c. 1 in.
  d. 4 in.

44. In a dwelling unit, a minimum of _____ VA per square foot shall be allocated for the general lighting load.
  a. 1
  b. 2
  c. 3
  d. 5

45. Overhead service conductors and their specific clearance requirements can be found in Article/Section _____.
  a. 230.24
  b. 250
  c. 338.10
  d. 547

46. Handhole enclosures used in underground systems shall be _____.
 a. identified
 b. buried at least 36 inches
 c. provided with a manufactured bottom plate
 d. sized for personnel to enter

47. Which of the following NEC Articles covers overcurrent protective devices?
 a. 100
 b. 200
 c. 240
 d. 500

48. Which of the following NEC Sections would an electrician use to choose the grounding electrode conductors for a service?
 a. 250.122
 b. 250.66
 c. 310.8
 d. 680.26

49. Which one of the following statements about indoor spas and hot tubs is NOT accurate?
 a. Receptacles shall be at least 4 ft., measured horizontally, from the inside walls of the spa or hot tub.
 b. Receptacles that are rated 125 volts and 30 amperes or less and that are within 10 ft. of the inside walls of a spa or hot tub require GFCIs.
 c. Switches shall be at least 5 ft., measured horizontally, from the inside walls of the spa or hot tub.
 d. All of the above

50. A fuse or an overcurrent trip unit of a circuit breaker shall be connected in series with each _____.
 a. circuit breaker
 b. ungrounded conductor
 c. three-phase leg
 d. grounded conductor

51. Adjacent runs of heating cables shall be installed in accordance with _____.
 a. the National Electrical Code
 b. the authority having jurisdiction
 c. the manufacturer's instructions
 d. All of the above

52. A kitchen island requires at least one receptacle when
 a. any side of the island is longer than 3 ft.
 b. the countertop space has a long dimension of 24" or greater and a short dimension of 12" or greater.
 c. the island has a sink.
 d. None of the above

53. NEC Article _____ provides a backdrop for the introduction and scope of the NEC.
 a. Informative Annex A
 b. 90
 c. 100
 d. 220

54. The person responsible for starting, stopping, and controlling an amusement ride or supervising a concession is the
 a. operator.
 b. jurisdiction.
 c. ride or event guard.
 d. controller.

55. A 1-HP, single-phase AC motor at 208 V has a full load current of _____.
 a. 8.0 amps
 b. 8.8 amps
 c. 9.2 amps
 d. 16 amps

56. Requirements for transformer ventilation appear in which Section of the NEC?
 a. 225.3
 b. 240.4
 c. 300.1
 d. 450.9

57. The handles or escutcheon areas of circuit breakers rated at _____ amperes or less and _____ volts or less should be molded, stamped, etched, or similarly marked with their ampere ratings.
 a. 75
 b. 80
 c. 90
 d. 100

 a. 150
 b. 300
 c. 600
 d. 1,000

58. A 65-volt generator driven by a single motor is protected by the overcurrent device only while the generator is delivering less than _____ percent of its full-load rated current.
 a. 100
 b. 125
 c. 150
 d. 175

59. The branch circuit overcurrent protective device for conductors shall not exceed _____ amperes when the control circuit conductor for the motor is No. 10 AWG copper and doesn't extend beyond the motor control enclosure.
 a. 120
 b. 160
 c. 175
 d. 250

60. An inverse time circuit breaker is selected for a 60-HP, 460-V, 3-Phase AC, wound-rotor-type motor. The circuit breaker's maximum ampere rating shall not exceed _____ percent, in accordance with the motor's branch circuit, short circuit, and ground-fault protective device requirements.
 a. 150
 b. 250
 c. 300
 d. 600

61. Panelboards in damp or wet locations shall be installed to comply with Section _____.
 a. 312.2
 b. 314.15
 c. 408.17
 d. 110.28

62. Type TC cable with an outside diameter of 1 in. or less has a minimum bending radius of _____ the overall diameter of the cable.
 a. 4 times
 b. 5 times
 c. 6 times
 d. 12 times

63. Where service entrance cable with ungrounded conductors sizes 10 AWG and smaller are used on interior wiring and come in contact with thermal insulation, the ampacity shall be in accordance with the _____ conductor temperature rating.
 a. 90°C
 b. 120°C
 c. 140°F
 d. 167°F

64. Within 210.8 (A) through (E), the GFCI protection in those specific locations shall be _____.
a. identified for its specific use
b. readily accessible
c. accessible
d. within sight

65. The maximum total voltage drop percentage recommended on a branch circuit is _____.
a. 1
b. 2
c. 3
d. 5

66. There shall be no fewer than _____ small appliance branch circuit(s) serving the receptacles, as required in Section 210.52(B).
a. 1
b. 2
c. 3
d. 4

67. A feeder disconnect that is fed from a solidly grounded wye system of 1000 amps or more and more than 150 volts to ground, while not exceeding 600 volts between phases, shall be provided with _____.
a. ground-fault protection
b. AFCI protection
c. surge protection
d. GFCI protection

68. Service conductors installed to a building or other structure shall not _____ any other building(s) or structure(s).
a. be within 3 ft. of
b. pass through the interior of
c. be buried underneath
d. be grouped with service disconnects of

69. The disconnecting means for a building or structure supplied by a feeder shall be installed at a location that is considered _____, according to the NEC.
a. exposed
b. enclosed
c. guarded
d. readily accessible

70. When the electrician installs nonmetallic raceways (such as type PVC) underground without any concrete encasement, a minimum depth of cover shall be _____.
a. 4 inches
b. 8 inches
c. 12 inches
d. 18 inches

71. During the backfill process of an underground wiring installation, the electrician shall make sure the backfill material won't _____.
a. damage raceways, cables, or substructures
b. prevent adequate compaction of fill material
c. contain large rocks or corrosive materials
d. All of the above

72. When using directional boring equipment, cables, or raceways, they shall be _____ for the purpose.
a. labeled T
b. evaluated
c. approved
d. None of the above

73. When cable armors, cable sheaths, and metal or nonmetallic raceways are installed between cabinets, boxes, fittings, or other enclosures or outlets, they shall be _____, not including any exceptions.
a. identical in diameter
b. color coded or labeled
c. insulated or covered
d. continuous

74. Conductors that are installed in raceways between outlets, boxes, devices, and so forth shall be _____.
a. continuous
b. copper
c. copper or aluminum
d. no less than 14 AWG

75. For a shore power connection, the disconnection means shall be not more than _____ inches from the receptacle that it controls.
a. 24
b. 30
c. 32
d. 48

76. Feeder and service loads associated with fixed electric space heating shall be calculated at _____ percent of the total connected load.
a. 80
b. 100
c. 125
d. 150

77. When a motor disconnecting means is also a motor-circuit switch, the switch must be rated in _____.
a. voltage
b. amperes
c. horsepower
d. wattage

78. For a motor controller, the disconnection means shall be designed so that it cannot be _____ automatically.
a. isolated
b. opened
c. locked
d. closed

79. The maximum PV source circuit current shall be the sum of parallel module-rated short circuits multiplied by _____ percent.
a. 80
b. 100
c. 115
d. 125

80. A PV inverter's maximum output circuit current shall be equal to the _____ output current rating.
a. marked
b. continuous
c. instantaneous
d. volt-ampere

Practice Test 1
Answers and Explanations

1. The correct answer is choice **a**. In accordance with the minimum requirements of the National Electrical Code, the minimum thickness of $\frac{1}{16}$ in. is required, unless a thinner steel plate that has been marked or labeled for this specific use provides equal or better protection. $\frac{1}{8}$ in., $\frac{3}{8}$ in., and $\frac{1}{2}$ in. thick steel plates would exceed the minimum thickness and technically be permitted by the NEC. However, they would not be practical due to the thickness and would create a bowing affect in the finished gypsum board or similar finish. (NEC 300.4(A)(2))

2. The correct answer is **c**. In accordance with the minimum requirements of the National Electrical Code, direct-buried conductors and cables that emerge from grade shall be protected to a height above grade of 8 feet. This provides the needed protection against potential physical damage of emerging conductors and cables from finished grade. (NEC 300.5(D)(1))

3. The correct answer is **b**. The question asked for the minimum separation from the bottom of the electrical distribution equipment. The National Electrical Code gives a specific minimum requirement of 24 in. While choices **a**, **c**, and **d** are acceptable in the field, they are not the best possible answers for this question. (NEC 550.11(A))

4. The correct answer is **c**. In accordance with Section 240.4(D)(1), the overcurrent protection of an 18 AWG copper conductor shall not exceed 7 amperes. A conductor that was limited to 2 or 5 amperes would not be practical in terms of providing any specific use. A conductor rated 10 amperes would exceed the specific maximum ampere rating and overcurrent protection. (NEC 240.4(D)(1))

5. The correct answer is **d**. The maximum length for a kitchen waste disposer cord is 36 in. (NEC 422.16(B)(1)(2)). Choice **a** would be insufficient given the distance between a typical kitchen waste disposal and the dedicated receptacle outlet. It is far less than the minimum cord length requirement and nowhere near the maximum length permitted. The use of a 12-in. cord would be a violation of the National Electrical Code, as it is less than the minimum required length of cord. However, the question asked for the maximum length of the cord, and this answer is even less than the minimum required length. The use of a 24-in. cord would not be a violation of the National Electrical Code. However, the question asked for the maximum length of the cord. (NEC 422.16(B)(1)(2))

6. The correct answer is **a**. The allowable ampacity of an insulated conductor like THHN (heat-resistant thermoplastic insulation) is specified in Table 310.15(B)(16) and is only a starting point for properly sizing a conductor to a desired ampacity. Other factors like ambient temperatures and number of current carrying conductors in a cable or raceway can affect the final calculated ampacity of a conductor. Choice **b** has to do with cords; THHN is an individual conductor and not a cord. Choice **c** has to do with elevators and what conductors can actually be used in raceways or cables in elevator applications. The answer provides no guidance on allowable ampacity. Choice **d** has nothing to do with guidelines for ampacity values of THHN conductors; it provides guidance for bus or conductor ampere ratings for a specific application and provides no guidance for THHN. (NEC 310.15(B)(16))

7. The correct answer is **a**. In accordance with the 2017 NEC, a motor controller that is $\frac{1}{3}$ HP or less can be controlled by an attachment plug and receptacle or cord connector versus being hard wired. Any portable motor with a horsepower rating higher than $\frac{1}{3}$ will not permit the controller to be an attachment plug and receptacle or code connector. (NEC 430.81(B))

8. Choice **d** is correct. In accordance with the 2017 NEC, the capacity (in amperes) for circuit conductors associated with capacitors shall be not less than 135% of the rated current of the capacity. (NEC 460.8(A))

9. The correct answer is **b**. When considering parallel conductors for each phase, Section 310.10(H)(2) does not address the color of the insulation. Section 310.10(H)(2)(3) is very specific about maintaining characteristics that, if changed, could result in an improper division of current on the paralleled conductors of that phase. (NEC 310.10(H)(2)(3))

10. The correct answer is **d**. RHH-type thermoset insulation is rated for 194°F as its maximum operating temperature per Table 310.104(A). Limiting RHH-type insulation (thermoset) to 32°C or 60°C would limit its application uses and not maximize its industry potential for use. Typical device terminals are rated for 75°C; if limited to 32°C or 60°C, they would not be practical for everyday use. Typical device terminals are rated for 75°C; if limited to 75°F, they would translate into 23.89°C, which would not be practical for everyday use. (NEC 310.104(A))

11. The correct answer is **b**. According to section 590.4(C), type NM cable can be used for temporary purposes in dwellings, buildings, or structures with no height limitations only as long as they are protected from overcurrent, as provided in Sections 240.4, 240.5, and 240.100 where applicable. Choice **a** is incorrect because while Section 334.10(3) does not appear on the surface to impose height restrictions for use of type NM cable in buildings as long as they are type III, IV, and V construction, height for these construction types is limited in accordance with the International Building Code. The question is about removing these specific limitations for temporary applications. Question **c** is incorrect because 830.40(B) has nothing to do with nonmetallic-sheathed cable. (NEC 590.4(C))

12. The correct answer is **a**. When a term or phrase is used in more than one Article throughout the NEC, it is moved to Article 100, where definitions are found. Since the question asks for a definition, the only accurate choice is **a**. None of the other answer choices provide definitions. Choices **b**, **c**, and **d** have nothing to do with electrical phrases or definitions. (NEC 100)

13. The correct answer is **b**. Spaces used exclusively as patient sleeping rooms in nursing homes are removed from the more stringent requirements of Part II in Article 517. (NEC 517.10(B)(2)) Examining rooms are subject to requirements related to the examination and treatment of patients. Choice **a** is incorrect because this location is not included in the list of spaces provided in Section 517.10(B)(1) that remove the more stringent requirements in Part II of Article 517 for healthcare facilities. (NEC 517.10(B)(2)) Wet procedure spaces are subject to requirements related to the treatment of patients. Choice **c** is incorrect because this location is not included in the list of spaces provided in Section 517.10(B)(1) that remove the more stringent requirements in Part II of Article 517 for healthcare facilities. (NEC 517.10(B)(2)) Choice **d** is incorrect because treatment rooms are subject to requirements related to the active medical treatment of patients. This location is not included in the list of spaces provided in Section 517.10(B)(2) that remove the more stringent requirements in Part II of Article 517 for healthcare facilities. (NEC 517.10(B)(1))

14. The correct answer is **d**. The receptacle has a double volume allowance of the largest conductor attached to it, in accordance with 314.16(B)(4), and each individual conductor has a value of 2.00 cubic inches, per Table 314.16(B), including only one allowance for the equipment grounding conductor(s) per 314.16(B)(5). The total count is 5 conductors and a receptacle, which counts as 2 conductors, for a total of 7 conductors × 2.00 cubic inches, equaling 14 cubic inches. (NEC 314.16(B))

15. The correct answer is **c**. In existing installations where insulation is not a factor due to the original construction of the structure, the extension of knob-and-tube wire from already existing installations is permitted, provided it is not being installed in locations specified in Section 394.12. The NEC indirectly prohibits the use of knob-and-tube wiring methods in new installations and construction due to the insulating requirements for walls, ceilings, and attics in the residential and commercial building codes and energy conservation codes. Due to this being an open wiring system, it needs air to dissipate heat from current flowing within the conductor. (NEC 394.10)

16. The correct answer is **b**. The use of Table 250.122 is critical for the safe and reliable operation of an overcurrent protective device in a ground-fault condition because it lists the sizes of the equipment grounding conductors. Choice **a** is incorrect because this table is used to determine the size of grounded conductors, main bonding jumpers, systems bonding jumpers, and supply-side bonding jumpers. It has nothing to do with sizing the equipment grounding conductor. Choice **c** is incorrect because this table is used to size the grounding electrode conductors for a building's grounding electrode system. It has nothing to do with sizing the equipment grounding conductors. Choice **d** is incorrect because this table provides the allowable ampacities of insulated conductors under specific conditions. It has nothing to do with sizing the equipment grounding conductors. (NEC Table 250.122)

17. The correct answer is **a**. According to Ohm's Law, E = I × R. Therefore; the applied voltage (E) equals total current (I) multiplied by the total resistance (R). E = 6 amperes × 20 ohms = 120 volts. An answer of 12 volts would result from an arithmetic error of not carrying the decimal point far enough to the right. An answer of 3.33 volts would result from applying the formula incorrectly, that of E = R ÷ I or 20 amperes ÷ 6 ohms = 3.33 volts. An answer of 0.3 volts would result in applying the formula incorrectly, that of E = I ÷ R or 6 ohms ÷ 20 amperes = 0.3 volts.

18. The correct answer is **a**. Due to the "on and off" activity of elevators, demand factors can be applied for multiple motors versus the traditional sizing requirements in 620.13(D). According to section 620.14, that demand factor is 0.77 due to 7 elevator motors running at random times, which can be applied to reduce the size of the feeder. The values in choices **b** and **c** do not appear in Table 620.14 as an option. Choice **d** would not provide any demand factor since it is 100%. This is already provided for in Section 620.13(D), where no demand factors have been applied. (NEC 620.14)

19. The correct answer is **c**. As defined in Article 100, a continuous load is a load where the maximum current is expected to continue for 3 hours or longer. Contiguous is defined as being in actual contact or touching along a specific boundary, which has nothing to do with power being supplied for at least 3 hours. The term half-day does not depict the actual use or duration of load activity. Choice **d** has nothing to do with the correct term for this kind of load. (NEC 100)

20. The correct answer is C. Not only does a ground ring have to be no less than 30 inches below the Earth's surface, it also has to completely surround the structure or building, creating a lasso-type effect. (NEC 250.53(F))

21. The correct answer is **d**. The motors, controllers, and wiring of electrically operated pool covers shall not be less than 5 ft. from the inside wall of the pool unless they are separated from the pool by a wall, a cover, or another permanent barrier. (NEC 680.27(B)(1))

22. The correct answer is **b**. In accordance with Section 210.11(C)(3), the minimum size branch circuit for the required receptacle(s) per Section 210.52(D) is 20 amperes. Section 210.11(C)(3) is very specific about the minimum branch circuit size required to supply the receptacles that meet Section 210.52(D). 15, 25, and 30 amps are not specified in the code reference (NEC 210.11(C)(3)).

23. The correct answer is **c**. In accordance with Section 250.64(A), aluminum grounding electrode conductors are required to maintain no less than 18 inches of physical separation from the Earth at termination to the grounding electrode. (NEC 250.64(A))

24. The correct answer is **b**. In electrical systems, you have either grounded or ungrounded systems to contend with. This section details the grounding and bonding requirements for ungrounded systems; knowing these details is critical to ensuring the safe and reliable operation of an ungrounded type system. The other choices have nothing to do with underground systems. (NEC 250.4(B))

25. The correct answer is **c**. The symbol "S_3" on a plan or diagram indicates a 3-way switch, which is suitable for controlling a load from two different locations. The symbol "S" on a plan or diagram indicates a single-pole switch, which is not suitable for controlling a load from two different locations. The symbol "S_2" on a plan or diagram indicates a double-pole switch, which is not suitable for controlling a load from two different locations. The symbol "S_4" on a plan or diagram indicates a 4-way switch, which is not suitable for controlling a load from two different locations. (ANSI)

26. The correct answer is **b**. Per Section 386.56, the NEC states that the installer shall not exceed 75% of area when splicing and taping conductors in surface metal raceways. Choice **a** is incorrect because the question is directed toward surface metal raceways and not cabinets, cutout boxes, or meter enclosures. While the 75% rule does exist in this section, it is not germane to the question. Choice **c** is incorrect because Section 398.3 does not exist in the NEC. Choice **d** is incorrect because the question is directed toward surface metal raceways and not cabinets, cutout boxes, or meter enclosures. While the 75% rule does exist in this section, it is not germane to the question. (NEC 386.56)

27. The correct answer is **b**. When performing calculations, Article 220 is the key place to explore. For farm loads, the NEC provides for diversity in electrical loads by allowing a demand factor to be applied, as permitted by Section 220.103. Choice **a** has nothing to do with demand factors; it provides a summary of various branch circuit requirements in Article 210. Choice **c** has nothing to do with demand factors. C.11(A) is a table located in the informative annex of the NEC; it shows the maximum number of conductors or fixture wires in rigid PVC conduit. (NEC 220.103)

28. The correct answer is **b**. Class II refers to dust-related conditions, and the question relates to combustible dust. Division II location indicates that combustible dust may be stored in such areas, yet the concentrations are not high enough to produce an explosion or become ignitable unless something abnormal takes place. Choice **a** is incorrect because Class I location is flammable gases, vapors, and combustible liquid-produced vapors and Division I location would have ignitable concentrations of combustible dust in the air under normal conditions, not under the abnormal conditions stated in the question. Choice **c** is incorrect because Class III location is for easily ignitable fibers and combustible flyings and Division III does not exist. Choice **d** is incorrect because Class IV and Division IV do not exist. (NEC 500.5(C)(2))

29. The correct answer was choice **b**. This is the only answer that specifically attempts to give guidance on reducing electronic noise, also known as EMF, on the grounding circuit. Choice **a** references the sizing of an equipment grounding conductor and offers no assistance in reducing electronic noise. Choice **c** provides no assistance in terms of reducing electronic noise and isolated receptacles. Choice **d** references grounding and bonding procedures for information technology rooms and does not respond to the question. (NEC 250.146(D))

30. The correct answer is **c**. NEC Article 424 sets out the requirements for fixed electric space-heating equipment. NEC Article 210 addresses branch circuits. NEC Article 422 addresses appliances. NEC Article 427 addresses fixed electric heating equipment for pipelines and vessels. (NEC 424)

31. The correct answer is **b**. Load calculations for services and feeders in commercial and industrial buildings require a specific volt-ampere value for each single receptacle or multiple receptacles per yoke, commonly also called a strap. Section 220.14(I) provides for 180 VA per yoke. 120 volt-amperes would be too low for calculation accuracy in accordance with Section 220.14(I), and 240 or 360 volt-amperes would be too excessive. (NEC 220.14(I))

32. The correct answer is **a**. According to Section Table 300.5 of the NEC, if the branch circuit is for dwelling-related purposes, the minimum burial depth shall be 18 inches. If the circuit had been GFCI protected, 120 volts, and protected by maximum overcurrent protection of 20 amperes, then the depth of burial cover could have been reduced to 12 inches. While burial of 24 inches would be acceptable, it is not the best answer since the minimum burial cover is 18 inches. The additional 6 inches would not offer any enhanced level of cable protection. (NEC Table 300.5)

33. The correct answer is **d**. Insulation temperature limitations is not one of the required markings on heating cables. The other choices are all requirements. (NEC 424.35)

34. The correct answers are **a** and **d**. Article 240 addresses overcurrent protection; cartridge fuses are one specific type of protective device. Part VI addresses overcurrent protection, and cartridge fuses are the specific type of protective device being discussed in Part VI. Article 300 addresses the various wiring methods and materials for electrical installations and has nothing to do with rules governing cartridge fuses. Article 430 addresses motors and has nothing to do with rules governing cartridge fuses. Article 500 addresses hazardous locations for electrical installations and has nothing to do with rules governing cartridge fuses. Part II of Article 240 addresses the locations of overcurrent protective devices such as fuses or circuit breakers and is not specifically dedicated to cartridge fuses. Part III of Article 240 addresses enclosures for overcurrent protective devices and is not specifically dedicated to cartridge fuses. Part IV of Article 240 addresses disconnecting and guarding for fuses and is not specifically dedicated to cartridge fuses. (NEC 240, Part VI)

35. The correct answer is **b**. Chapter 6 of the NEC is titled Special Equipment; this article addresses the use of audio-signal processing equipment. Chapter 5 of the NEC is titled Special Occupancies. Chapter 7 of the NEC is titled Special Conditions, such as emergency power needs or specialized classes of low voltage wiring, and is not related to equipment. (NEC 640)

36. The correct answer is **d**. FEP, FEPB, MTW, PFA, THHN, THHW, THWN, and a host of other insulated conductor types are allowed in dry/ damp locations. (NEC 310.10(B))

37. The correct answer is **b**. A receptacle outlet shall be installed at each wall countertop and work surface space that is 12 inches or wider. Choice **a** is incorrect. While 14 and 18 inches are wider, it is not the minimum diminution expressed in Section 210.52(C)(1). (NEC 210.52(C)(1))

38. The correct answers are **b** and **b**. As stated in Section 320.30, type AC cable shall be secured within 12 in. of every outlet box, junction box, cabinet, or fitting and at intervals not exceeding $4\frac{1}{2}$ ft. where installed on or across framing members. (NEC 320.30)

39. The correct answer is **c**. This requirement is to ensure that at any point on the wall a receptacle outlet will be available for use with various cord-and-plug-connected equipment. The standard length of cord for a floor lamp is 6ft. This rule also helps discourage the use of extension cords due to the lack of receptacle outlets available. Choice **a** is incorrect because 2 ft. is below the minimum requirement. Choice **b** is incorrect because you can go above code, but 6 ft. from any point on the wall line is the minimum code requirement. Choice **d** is incorrect because 12 ft. would encourage the use of extension cords due to a lack of available receptacle outlets. (NEC 210.52(A)(1))

40. The correct answer is **c**. Section 517.19(B)(2) requires that the grounding terminal of each hospital-grade receptacle installed in the patient bed locations within the critical care areas of healthcare facilities shall be connected to the reference grounding point by means of an insulated copper equipment grounding conductor. Choice **a** is incorrect because Section 517.19(B)(2) requires that the grounding terminal of each receptacle shall be connected to the reference grounding point by means of an insulated copper equipment grounding conductor, not a bare equipment grounding conductor. Choice **b** is incorrect because having a conductor one gauge larger would not satisfy this question or the NEC requirement. The only option that is accurate is **c**, based on the language of Section 517.19(B)(2). (NEC 517.19(B)(2))

41. The correct answer is **d**. The 2014 NEC experienced a few changes in the requirements for AFCI protection of branch circuits. The NEC added both kitchens and laundry areas to the list of locations where specific branch circuits now require AFCI protection. Bedrooms are included in the list of locations where specific branch circuits require AFCI protection. (NEC 210.12(A))

42. The correct answer is **c**. Where they are within 3.0 m (10 ft.) of any building or structure other than supporting poles or towers, open individual (aerial) overhead conductors shall be insulated for the nominal voltage. Choice **a** is incorrect because providing only 5 ft. of conductor covering would not meet the minimum code requirements. Choice **b** is incorrect because providing only 6 ft. of conductor covering would not meet the minimum code requirements. Choice **d** is incorrect because providing only 25 ft. of conductor covering would exceed the minimum code requirements. (NEC 225.4)

43. The correct answer is **d**. As stated in Section 225.14(C), open conductors shall be separated from open conductors of other circuits or systems by not less than 100 mm (4 in.). Choice **a** is incorrect because 50 mm, which is approximately 2 in., would not be code compliant. Choice **b** is incorrect because while 200 mm, approximately 8 in., would be field acceptable and would meet code, it doesn't provide the best possible answer to the question, which asks for a minimum separation value. Choice **c** is incorrect because 1 in. would not be code compliant. (NEC 225.14(C))

44. The correct answer is **c**. In accordance with Section 220.12 and Table 220.12, dwelling units shall be calculated at 3 VA per square foot for their general lighting loads when doing service and feeder calculations, not including open porches, garages, or unused or unfinished spaces not adaptable for future use. Choice **a** is incorrect because 1 VA per square foot would not adequately provide for the needed electrical capacity to handle general lighting loads. Choice **b** is incorrect because 2 VA per square foot would not adequately provide for the needed electrical capacity to handle general lighting loads. Choice **d** is incorrect because 5 VA would only serve to oversize the service. While 5 VA is not a NEC violation, it is considered excessive. (NEC 220.12)

45. The correct answer is **a**. This is the section for clearances of overhead service conductors. Overhead service conductors shall not be readily accessible and shall comply with 230.24(A) through (E) for services not over 1,000 volts, nominal. Choice **b** is incorrect because Article 250 is for grounding and bonding applications and has nothing to do with overhead service conductors or clearances. Choice **c** is incorrect because Article 338 has nothing to do with overhead service conductors or clearances. Section 338.10 addresses permitted uses of service-entrance cable. Choice **d** is incorrect because Article 547 is for agricultural buildings only and has nothing to do with overhead service conductors or clearances. (NEC 230.24)

46. The correct answer is **a**. As stated in Section 314.3, handhole enclosures shall be designed and installed to withstand all loads likely to be imposed on them. They shall be identified for use in underground systems. Choice **b** is incorrect because due to the nature of a handhole, placing them 36 in. in the Earth would make them useless. Choice **c** is incorrect because the nature of a handhole enclosure is to have an open bottom or closed bottom depending on the model and design; neither requires a manufactured bottom plate in order to be used underground. Choice **d** is incorrect because handhole enclosures shall be designed and installed to withstand all loads likely to be imposed on them. They shall be identified for use in underground systems. The intent of a handhold enclosure is to reach into it by hand. (NEC 314.30)

47. The correct answer is **c**. Article 240 is the primary location to find information on overcurrent protective devices. Choice **a** is incorrect because Article 100 has definitions for common electrical terms and phrases used more than once throughout the NEC. Choice **b** is incorrect because Article 200 addresses the use and identification of grounded conductors and has nothing to do with overcurrent protective devices. Choice **d** is incorrect because Article 500 addresses hazardous locations and has nothing to do with overcurrent protective devices. (NEC 240)

48. The correct answer is **b**. When sizing the grounding electrode conductor (GEC), Section 250.66 offers the correct method of determining the proper sizes. Choice **a** is incorrect because Section 250.122 is used to size equipment grounding conductors; they are selected based on the size of the overcurrent protection device protecting the circuit. Choice **c** is incorrect because Section 310.8 does not exist. Choice **d** is incorrect because Section 680.28 is used when establishing an equipotential bonding around pools. (NEC 250.66)

49. The correct answer is **a**. Receptacles are required to be no less than 6 ft. from the inside wall of the spa or hot tub. For indoor spas and hot tubs, the code section is 680.43(A)(1). Choice **b** is incorrect because the NEC requires GFCI protection on receptacles rated 30 amperes or less that are also 125 volts. Choice **c** is incorrect because while Part IV specifically addresses spas and hot tubs, Section 680.43 will remind the installer that Part I and II are still in play for indoor spas and hot tubs. Section 680.22(C) demands 5 ft. separation from the inside wall of the pool unless otherwise separated by a barrier such as a fence or other permanent barrier. (NEC 480.43(A)(1))

50. The correct answer is **b**. As stated in Section 240.15(A), a fuse or an overcurrent trip unit of a circuit breaker shall be connected in series with each ungrounded conductor. By placing overcurrent protection in series with the ungrounded conductor, the device is perfectly placed to prevent damage to the conductors in an overload, short-circuit, and ground fault condition. Choice **a** is incorrect because as stated in Section 240.15(A), a fuse or an overcurrent trip unit of a circuit breaker shall be connected in series with each ungrounded conductor, not a circuit breaker. By placing overcurrent protection in series with the ungrounded conductor, the device is perfectly placed to prevent damage to the conductors in an overload, short-circuit, and ground fault condition. Choice **c** is incorrect because as stated in Section 240.15(A), a fuse or an overcurrent trip unit of a circuit breaker shall be connected in series with each ungrounded conductor. By placing overcurrent protection in series with the ungrounded conductor, the device is perfectly placed to prevent damage to the conductors in an overload, short-circuit, and ground fault condition. Choice **d** is incorrect because Section 240.22 prohibits the placement of overcurrent protective devices in series with any conductor that is intentionally grounded. The very nature of the term *grounded conductor* shows that it is intentionally grounded at the source. While there are a few permitted allowances, the general rule is, no OCPD in series with grounded conductors. (NEC 240.15(A))

51. The correct answer is **c**. As stated in Section 424.44(A), adjacent runs of heating cables shall be installed in accordance with the manufacturer's instructions. (NEC 424.44(A))

52. The correct answer is **b**. The need for a receptacle for supplying power to appliances at an island is covered by the requirements of Section 210.52(C)(2). When the countertop space has a long dimension of 24" or more and a short dimension of 12" or more, the desire to use the surface area is greater, and having a receptacle reduces the desire to use extension cords. Choice **a** is incorrect because the requirement for having at least one receptacle to serve the countertop space of an island has nothing to do with the side of the island. It is the countertop area that defines the need for a receptacle per Section 210.52(C)(2). Choice **c** is incorrect because the requirement for having at least one receptacle to serve the countertop space of an island has nothing to do with the side of the island. Choice **d** is incorrect because the requirement for having at least one receptacle to serve the countertop space of an island has nothing to do with the sink in terms of the minimum receptacle requirements. However, if the sink divides up the countertop space into two separate countertops that meet the minimum size requirements of Section 210.52(C)(2), then additional receptacles may be required for each island countertop space. (NEC 210.52(C)(2))

53. The correct answer is **b**. Article 90 is the introduction to the NEC. It defines what is covered and what is not covered within the document. This article also lays out the intended scope and code layout structure for each article and section. Choice **a** is incorrect because the Informative Annexes within the NEC include additional information that is not required by the NEC. The annexes are a great resource but are not code enforceable. Annex A provides a detailed list of code standards associated with the various code articles and sections within the NEC. Choice **c** is incorrect because Article 100 has definitions for common electrical terms and phrases used throughout the NEC. Choice **d** is incorrect because Article 220 is used for branch circuit, feeder, and service calculations only. It is not there to be an introduction or explain the scope of the NEC's intent. (NEC 90)

54. The correct answer is **a**. The operator is the person responsible for starting, stopping, and controlling an amusement ride or supervising a concession. Choice **b** is incorrect because the jurisdiction still falls under the locality where the event is taking place. Choice **c** is incorrect because technically speaking, the operator is not a guard of anything. He or she is not in a position to deny access to the rides or concessions but has a responsibility to stop, start, and control the flow of the ride or concessions area. Choice **d** is incorrect because the operator is the person responsible for starting, stopping, and controlling an amusement ride or supervising a concession. (NEC 525.2)

55. The correct answer is **b**. The FLC of a 208-V single-phase motor of 1 HP is 8.8 amps. Choice **a** is incorrect because 8.0 amps is not accurate in terms of the FLC for a 1-HP single-phase motor. Choice **c** is incorrect because 9.2 is not accurate in terms of the FLC for a 1-HP single-phase motor. Choice **d** is incorrect because 16 is not accurate in terms of the FLC for a 1-HP single-phase motor. (NEC Table 430.248)

56. The correct answer is **d**. This section details the requirements for transformer ventilation. The ventilation shall dispose of the transformer full-load heat losses without creating a temperature rise that is in excess of the transformer rating. Choices **a**, **b**, and **c** are incorrect because these sections have nothing to do with transformers or ventilation. (NEC 450.9)

57. The correct answers are **d** and **d**. As stated in Section 240.83(B), the handles or escutcheon areas of circuit breakers rated at 100 amperes or less and 1,000 volts or less should be molded, stamped, etched, or similarly marked with their ampere ratings. (NEC 240.83(B))

58. The correct answer is **c**. Generators operating at 65 volts or less and driven by individual motors shall be considered as protected by the overcurrent protective device if these devices will operate when the generators are delivering not more than 150 percent of their full-load current. Choice **a** is incorrect because while 100 percent is less than 150 percent, it is not the best possible answer to the question. Choice **b** is incorrect because while 125 percent is less than 150 percent, it is not the best possible answer to the question. Choice **d** is incorrect because 175 percent is more than the 150 percent demanded to satisfy the NEC requirements. (NEC 445.12(C))

59. The correct answer is **b**. Section 430.72(B)(2) clearly permits the 160 amperes of protection for the conductors within the motor control enclosure that do not leave the enclosure. The values given in column B of Table 430.72(B) shall not be exceeded. Choices **c** and **d** are incorrect because the choice of 175 amps or 250 amps would exceed the value given in the table. Choice **a** is incorrect because the choice of 120 amps would not exceed the value given in the table but would not provide the best logical answer to the question. (NEC 430.72(B)(2))

60. The correct answer is **a**. The rating of the protective device that is to provide the short circuit and ground fault protection to the motor is required to be sized based on Table 430.52. The wound motor in the Inverse Trip Breaker column shows 150%. This would result in 77 amps × 150% = 116 amps. The protective device is not to exceed this value. Choices **b**, **c**, and **d** are incorrect because these answer choices exceed these values. (NEC 430.52(C)(1))

61. The correct answer is **a**. When installing a cabinet with a panelboard in a wet or damp location, the installer must visit Section 312.2 for guidance. Breaching the cabinet is the major concern when it comes to moisture getting into the equipment and onto the panelboard. (NEC 408.37)

62. The correct answer is **a**. Due to the overall diameter of the type TC cable being only 1 in., Section 336.24(A) requires that the minimum radius from the start to the end of the bend be no less than four times the overall diameter of the cable itself. Choice **b** is incorrect. It would be correct if the overall diameter of type TC cable was larger than 1 in. but less than 2 in. The correct answer is four times the overall diameter of the type TC cable. Choice **c** would only be correct if the overall diameter of type TC cable was larger than 2 in. Choice **d** would only be correct if the type TC cable had metallic shielding as part of its construction. (NEC 336.24(1))

63. The correct answer is **c**. As stated in Section 338.10(B)(4)(a), if a service entrance cable comes in contact with thermal insulation, the ampacity value is to be in accordance with the 60°C/140°F values found in Table 310.15(B)(16). While it is acceptable to use the higher insulation value for corrections and adjustments, the end ampacity value is not to exceed the 60°C or 140°F value. Choice **a** is incorrect because while it is acceptable to use the higher insulation value for corrections and adjustments, the end ampacity value is not to exceed the 60°C or 140°F value. 90°C is well above the permitted final ampacity values. Choice **b** is incorrect because 120°C is well above the permitted values. Choice **d** is incorrect because 167°F is the same as 75°C and is not in accordance with Section 338.10(B)(4)(a). (NEC 338.10(B)(4)(a))

64. The correct answer is **b**. Within 210.8 (A) through (E), the GFCI protection in those specific locations shall be readily accessible. Choice **a** is incorrect because typical GFCI devices are identified in accordance with UL943 for a specific ground-fault condition, and specific use listings are not needed. They are, however, required to be readily accessible for monthly testing, per the manufacturers' instructions. Choice **c** is incorrect because typical GFCI devices are identified in the charging statement of Section 210.8 as needing to be readily accessible; only being accessible would not facilitate quick and ready access to the device for testing in accordance with the device listings and manufacturer's instructions. Choice **d** is incorrect because while this is a good notion in itself, the device needs to remain readily accessible; being within sight is generally used in terms of a disconnection and means being within sight of a specific motor, appliance, or similar item under a specific condition of use.

65. The correct answer is **c**. While voltage drop is only a recommendation in terms of branch circuits and feeders, it is required in other areas of the NEC, like Fire Pumps (Article 695) and Sensitive Electrical Equipment (Article 647). Ensuring that the voltage remains within the parameters set by specific electrical equipment helps ensure proper operation and long service life. Choice **a** is incorrect because the informational note 4 of Section 210.19(A) recommends 3% for the branch circuit and 5% overall for both the branch and feeder. 1% is not the recommendation for a branch circuit. Choice **b** is incorrect because 2% is not the recommendation for a branch circuit. Choice **d** is incorrect because 5% is not the recommendation for a branch circuit. (NEC 210.19(A) *Informational Note 4*)

66. The correct answer is **b**. The NEC is specific about the minimum amount of small appliance branch circuits needed to serve the small appliance requirements. While more than 2 small appliance branch circuits can be installed as desired, the minimum required is 2. Choice **a** is incorrect because the minimum number of small appliance branch circuits needed to serve the small appliance requirements is 2. Choices **c** and **d** are incorrect; however, it is acceptable to exceed the minimums required by the NEC as along as you account for each circuit when doing your service and feeder load calculations found in Parts III and IV of Article 220. (NEC 210.11(C)(1))

67. The correct answer is **a**. As defined in Article 100 of the NEC, ground-fault protection of equipment provides needed protection of the equipment due to potential excessive line-to-ground fault currents. These devices are not circuit breakers or fuses designed to protect conductors; they are designed to protect the equipment and, in many cases, sensitive internal circuits. Choice **b** is incorrect because AFCI protection is mandated on branch circuits as described in Section 210.12(A) and (B). It has nothing to do with the feeder disconnect described in this question. Choice **c** is incorrect because although surge protection is very important and is described in detail in Article 285, it is not limited to 1,000 amps or more. See Article 285 for more details on surge-protective devices. Choice **d** is incorrect because GFCI protection is designed for personal protection of individuals and will activate at 6 mA and higher, but will not activate under 4 mA. The correct answer is AFCI protection because ground-fault protection is designed to function at a much higher mA value, typically 40 to 60 mA, depending on the manufacturer of the device, and is called GFP. (NEC 215.10)

68. The correct answer is **b**. Typically, service conductors supply a building or structure without any supply-side overcurrent protection. Section 230.70(A)(1) limits the amount of unprotected service conductors within a building or structure, and Section 230.3 serves to prohibit these unprotected conductors from going from one building or structure to another. Answer **a** is incorrect because being installed within 3 ft. of another building is very common with service conductors supplying a building or structure. In many cases, it is not possible to maintain such a separation from each building. The correct answer is *pass through the interior* because typically service conductors supply a building or structure without any supply-side overcurrent protection. Section 230.70(A)(1) limits the amount of unprotected service conductors within a building or structure, and Section 230.3 also prohibits these unprotected conductors from going from one building or structure to another. Choice **c** is incorrect because as long as the service conductors are considered outside of the building, they are permitted to pass underneath one building to another as needed, keeping in mind termination limitations expressed in Section 230.70(A)(1). The concern is with these service conductors passing through the interior of one building to another without any overcurrent protection. Choice **d** is incorrect because while grouping is important and is explained in detail in Section 230.72(A), since the question addresses two or more separate buildings, the service disconnects of each separate building or structure is not required to be grouped together. (NEC 230.3)

69. The correct answer is **d**. It is very important that everyone, including tenants, where applicable, have access to the disconnection means for each building or structure. This also permits a documented, readily accessible location for the disconnection means to be turned off as needed or placed in a safe position (open) when needed for servicing of the electrical system. Choice **a** is incorrect because being exposed is a good thing in terms of gaining access. However, the term *exposed* is too vague in terms of the specific requirement, which deals with a disconnection means location. See definitions in Article 100 to learn more about these very important terms. Choice **b** is incorrect because being enclosed is a requirement for disconnection means components to avoid contact with live parts. However, the term *enclosed* does not directly answer the location-specific requirement. Choice **c** is incorrect because as defined in the NEC, *being guarded* is used to describe placing electrical equipment in a guarded or protected state. In general, if the installer placed the disconnection means as guarded, it could potentially defeat the readily accessible provision. However, the term *guarded* does not directly answer the location-specific requirement. (NEC 225.32)

70. The correct answer is **d**. For a nonmetallic raceway that is not afforded the added protection of being encased in concrete, the minimum depth of cover is 18 inches. Choices **a**, **b**, and **c** are incorrect. There are other locations and conditions found in Table 300.5 where the depth could potentially see a depth of cover reduction depending on the specific locations described in the table. (NEC 300.5(A), Table 300.5; Column 3)

71. The correct answer is **d**. Each of the items must be taken into account to avoid the potential damage and degradation of the wiring method installed. Choices **a**, **b**, and **c** are incorrect because while these options are important and have to be considered, so do the other options. (NEC 300.5(F))

72. The correct answer is **c**. As stated in Section 354.10(1), the wiring methods that can be used with directional boring equipment must be approved by the local authority having jurisdiction. The term *approved* is a defined term found in Article 100 of the NEC. Article 354, Type NUCC Conduit, does identify its use with directional boring equipment in Section 354.10(1) for an example. Choice **a** is incorrect because while all raceways have to be listed and labeled as part of their product evaluation by the National Recognized Testing Laboratory (NRTL), the end result of the use of these products is determined by the authority having jurisdiction, which approves the installation method and material being used. Choice **b** is incorrect because while all raceways have to be listed and labeled and subsequently evaluated by the National Recognized Testing Laboratory (NRTL) for their applicable uses, the end result of the use of these products is determined by the authority having jurisdiction, which approves the installation method and material being used. Choice **d** is incorrect because, in accordance with Section 300.5(K), cables or raceways that are identified for use with directional boring equipment shall be approved for use with that equipment. Since a specific raceway or cable is not expressed in Chapter 3 of the NEC, which deals with wiring methods, the authority having jurisdiction will have to determine the approved wiring method based on documentation provided by the directional boring equipment manufacturer. (NEC 300.5(K))

73. The correct answer is **d**. As stated in Section 300.12, it is important that armors, sheathing, and raceways between cabinets, boxes, fittings, or other enclosures or outlets remain continuous except as permitted otherwise by the NEC. One of the exceptions to this general rule is when using a raceway as a sleeve for providing protection against physical damage to another wiring method that is not permitted to be subject to physical damage (i.e., nonmetallic-sheathed cable, type NM-B). Choice **a** is incorrect because this is not mandated on cable armors, sheathing, or raceways unless you are installing parallel conductors and wiring methods in accordance with Section 310.10(H). This requirement is more about the mechanical continuity of raceways and cables and less about the individual conductors themselves. Choice **b** is incorrect because while labeling is important and color-coding also has its place in terms of safety and good workmanship, it plays little role in the wiring method itself. For example, today, nonmetallic sheathed cable is color coded based on a voluntary industry move rather than a code-specific mandate, but this answer would not be appropriate for cables and raceways that typically do not have any surface markings, like RMC and IMC. Choice **c** is incorrect because while a raceway or cable can be covered or insulated as demanded by the specific need and use, it is not a requirement in general. For example, type MC (metal-clad cable) is typically not covered or insulated, but it is available as type MC–PVC jacketed or covered as an option for installation in a wet location where normal MC is prohibited. (NEC 300.12)

74. The correct answer is **a**. The solution here is to avoid splices and taps in raceways in general by keeping conductors installed continuously within such raceways, except where specifically permitted by the NEC, such as splices and taps in metal wireways in Article 376. Choice **b** is incorrect because while copper is generally the default conductor used within the NEC unless expressed otherwise, it is not the only conductor accepted for installation, as stated in Section 310.106(B). Choice **c** is incorrect because while copper is generally the default conductor used within the NEC unless expressed otherwise, and aluminum is usually chosen when weight and cost are factors to be considered, they are not the only conductors accepted for installation, as stated in Section 310.106(B). Copper-clad aluminum conductors are also an option where applicable. The question is about how conductors are installed in raceways to avoid splices and taps, except where specifically permitted by the NEC, such as metal wireways in Article 376. Choice **d** is incorrect because the smallest building wire permitted is given in Table 310.106(A), which indicates it should be 14 AWG if copper or 12 AWG if aluminum. However, the general statement of Section 310.106(A) says that conductors in general can be smaller where specifically permitted within the NEC, for example in Article 725 when working with Class 2 and 3 circuits, which are typically power limited and are sized typically 18 AWG to 16 AWG. Many other locations within the NEC permit smaller conductors where applicable. (NEC 300.13(A))

75. The correct answer is **b**. The NEC gives a set maximum distance that the disconnection means can't exceed, which is 30 inches from the receptacle controlled by the disconnect. Choice **a** is incorrect because while 24 inches is less than the 30-inch maximum distance, the question is asking for a specific maximum value. Choice **c** is incorrect because 32 inches would exceed that maximum value. Choice **d** is incorrect because 48 inches would exceed that maximum value. (NEC 555.17(B))

76. The correct answer is **b**. As stated in Section 220.51, the 100% connected load value of fixed space heating is to be used when performing a load calculation in Article 220. Choice **a** is incorrect because limiting the percentage to 80% would not provide all of the flexibility afforded when installing fixed electric space heating. Also, Section 220.51 states that the percentages permitted when performing the feeder and service calculations shall be taken at a value of 100% with few exceptions. Choices **c** and **d** are incorrect because sizing the fixed space heating loads at more than the 100% described in the NEC would result in needless oversizing or inflated load calculations that would result in larger conductors, overcurrent devices, and other electrical equipment that rely on accurate connected load values. While it is not a code violation, it may create a chain reaction where electrical material is oversized based on an inflated calculation. The NEC is a minimum code standard, and the 100 percent is the minimum given in Section 220.51. (NEC 220.51)

77. The correct answer is **c**. When working with motors, it is critical to know horsepower ratings when determining ampacity of a given motor. This is equally important when selecting motor-circuit switches to be used as disconnection means, as depicted in the question. Choices **a** and **b** are incorrect because since we are dealing with a motor switch, not only would it need to establish its voltage range in section 404.15(A), but the motor-circuit switch would also have to comply with Section 430.109(A)(1), which specifically requires the motor-control switch to be horsepower rated. Choice **d** is incorrect because wattage is not a value that is required for a switch. Wattage is a measurement of power and is usually associated with electrical equipment that consumes power rather than controls it. An example of this would be a standard 60-watt lamp; the wattage is a measurement of power and reflects the work being performed. (NEC 430.109(A)(1))

78. The correct answer is **d**. When installing a disconnection means, the last thing you would want is to have it close on its own, potentially energizing a circuit that someone may be working on, as this would defeat the intent of the disconnection means in the first place. For example, installing a knife-type disconnect incorrectly could cause the contact bars to close due to gravity and energize the circuit by itself. These types of disconnection means have specific designs and listing requirements to how they are installed to limit the potential of automatic closure. Anything can be isolated, but it does not have any anything to with the design of the disconnection means as stated in the question. In many areas of the NEC, disconnection means are required to be locked in the open position for various reasons, so any design that would produce a disconnection means for a motor controller and not have the ability to be locked would defeat the intent of Section 110.25–Lockable Disconnection Means. (NEC 430.103)

79. The correct answer is **d**. As stated in Section 690.8(A)(1)(1), each module will have a short-circuit current rating; installed in series, the short-circuit current does not increase, but you have to multiply the short-circuit current ratings by 125% to account for irradiance, also known as standard solar intensity, because the short-circuit current may increase beyond the modules' listed values depending on the time of day and position of the sun. Sizing to only 80%, 100%, or 115% would amount to installing a conductor that is undersized for the potential current it will be called to carry safely. (NEC 690.8(A)(1)(1))

80. The correct answer is **b**. The maximum currents on the output side of the inverter must be equal to the label that provides the continuous output current rating of the actual inverter to the AC system. (NEC 690.8(A)(3))

Questions answered correctly _____

Questions answered incorrectly _____

Passing score = minimum of 70%, or 56+ questions correctly.

3 ▶ PRACTICE TEST 2

This practice exam was designed to reflect the format, level, specifications, and content found on typical state tests for Journeyman Electrician certification/licensing. It contains questions based on the 2017 National Electrical Code and related electrical theory.

Official Journeyman Electrician examinations are typically open book tests. This means that you will be allowed to bring and reference any bound copy of the *National Electrical Code® 2017 Edition* during testing. You should also feel free to do so for this practice examination, but it is highly recommended that you check with your state's licensing board to confirm your state's specific testing requirements and allowances.

The official tests are typically four hours (240 minutes). If you would like to practice answering questions under test-like conditions, be sure to set a timer and take the exam in a quiet place where you will be undisturbed for the duration.

After you are finished, evaluate how you did with the answers and explanations immediately following the practice test. Your scores will be based on the number of questions you have answered correctly. A passing score is a minimum of 70%, so your goal is to answer a minimum of 56 questions correctly.

Good luck!

1. The National Electrical Code provides guidance for the installation and removal of electrical conductors, equipment, and raceways; signaling and communication conductors, equipment, and raceways; and optical fiber cables, raceways, and which of the following?
   a. underground mining installations
   b. ships and nautical wiring
   c. railways
   d. industrial sub-station

2. A(n)_____ is someone with skills and knowledge related to the construction and operation of equipment, as well as training to recognize and avoid the related hazards.
   a. electrical inspector
   b. AHJ representative
   c. job foreperson
   d. qualified person

3. In the circuit illustrated below, the three resistors are of equal value, each is rated at 45 ohms. Determine the total resistance of the circuit.

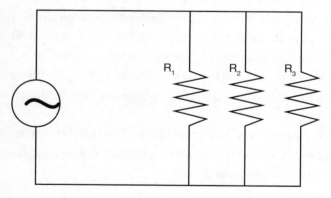

   a. 15 Ohms
   b. 45 Ohms
   c. 135 Ohms
   d. insufficient information to solve the problem

4. The applied voltage of the circuit illustrated in question number 3 equals 90 volts. The current through each resistor equals _____ amperes.
   a. 2
   b. 6
   c. 1,350
   d. 4,050

5. A _____ type of pipeline heating system uses induced current and hysteresis.
   a. resistance
   b. skin-effect
   c. induction
   d. impedance

6. All splices in electrical wiring must be covered with _____.
   a. duct tape
   b. insulation equivalent to that of the conductor
   c. a nonmetallic plate
   d. vinyl tape

7. According to NEC Section_____, illumination is required in all working spaces around service equipment, switchboards, switchgear, panel boards, and motor control centers installed indoors.
   a. 110.26(D)
   b. 210.70(A)(1)
   c. 408.16
   d. 410.16

8. Metal frames of switchgear and industrial control assemblies operating at more than 1,000 volts, nominal, shall be connected to a(n)_____ or, where permitted, the grounded conductor.
   a. current-limiting protective device
   b. nonmetallic base
   c. insulating material
   d. equipment grounding conductor

9. Receptacles as specified in NEC Article 647 may NOT be used for _____.
a. motors
b. lighting equipment
c. telecom equipment
d. computers

10. NEC Article_____ governs the installation of Class 1, 2, and 3 remote controls and signal circuits.
a. 330
b. 525
c. 725
d. 730

11. An aircraft hangar, including any adjacent, connecting areas, is classified as a Class 1, Division 2 or Zone 2 location up to how many inches above the floor?
a. 12
b. 18
c. 24
d. 48

12. A structure intended to mount a wet-niche luminaire in a pool or spa is called a _____.
a. wet mount
b. forming shell
c. moisture barrier
d. moisture shunt

13. Hydrogen is considered which class and group of material?
a. Class1, Group A
b. Class 2, Group A
c. Class1, Group B
d. Class 2, Group B

14. Optical fiber cabling requirements appear in which NEC article?
a. 600
b. 770
c. 800
d. 821

15. Class 1 remote-control and signaling circuits shall not exceed _____ volts.
a. 1,000
b. 600
c. 150
d. 30

16. Listed outlet boxes designed to support a ceiling-suspended fan that weighs more than _____ lbs. shall have a maximum weight-supporting allowance marked on the outlet box.
a. 75
b. 50
c. 35
d. 25

17. In dwelling unit kitchens, receptacle outlets installed for work surfaces, if located above the work surface, shall not be more than _____ above the countertop.
a. 12 in.
b. 18 in.
c. 20 in.
d. 24 in.

18. Which of the following is NOT considered a fountain?
a. reflection pool
b. display pool
c. drinking fountain
d. All of the above

19. When considering an effective grounding path for grounding electrode conductors and bonding jumpers that connect to grounding electrodes, which of the following statements is correct?
a. Insulated joints should be bonded.
b. Any equipment likely to be disconnected for repairs or replacement should be bonded.
c. Bonding jumpers should be long enough to allow equipment removal while retaining the grounding path's integrity.
d. All of the above.

20. The branch circuit conductors supplying one or more units of information technology equipment should have an ampacity not less than _____ % of the total connected load.
a. 125
b. 150
c. 175
d. 200

21. A recessed luminaire not identified for contact with insulation shall be not less than _____ from combustible materials.
a. $\frac{1}{4}$ in.
b. $\frac{1}{2}$ in.
c. $\frac{3}{4}$ in.
d. 1 in.

22. Intermediate metal conduit (IMC) with a 1-inch trade size has a metric designator of _____.
a. 27
b. 28
c. 30
d. 32

23. Trade size $\frac{1}{2}$ in. of ENT has a nominal internal diameter of _____.
a. 0.602 in.
b. 0.804 in.
c. 1.029 in.
d. 2.047 in.

24. An insulated THHN 10 AWG copper conductor in a dry location, before any adjustments or corrections, has a maximum allowable ampacity of _____ amps.
a. 10
b. 20
c. 30
d. 40

25. NEC Article _____ covers air conditioners and equipment with hermetic refrigeration.
a. 440
b. 450
c. 610
d. 625

26. Which of the following NEC tables summarizes branch circuit requirements?
a. 210.23(B)(3)
b. 210.24
c. 220.42
d. 830.47(C)

27. A continuous-duty power-resistor conductor must be rated at _____ % of full-load current.
a. 60
b. 80
c. 110
d. 125

28. _____ type conductors are not rated for a 90°C (194°F) maximum operating temperature.
a. THW-2
b. ZW-2
c. USE
d. RHH

29. According to the NEC, EMT use is allowed for which of the following?
a. where subject to severe physical damage
b. exposed work
c. luminaire support
d. in contact with dissimilar metals

30. Per NEC Section _____, electricians who are calculating ampacity for an over 600-volt feeder for a transformer should use the transformer's nameplate ratings.
a. 705.30(B)
b. 554.1
c. 450.5(A)(4)
d. 215.2(B)(1)

31. When installing more than three current-carrying conductors in a raceway or cable, electricians should consult NEC Section _____ to understand any adjustments that need to be applied.
a. 310.15(B)(2)(a)
b. 310.15(B)(3)(a)
c. 310.15(B)(7)
d. None of the above

32. ENT must be marked at intervals not to exceed _____ ft.
a. 12
b. 10
c. 6
d. 4

33. Single-throw knife switches must be installed so that _____ will not tend to close them.
a. gravity
b. inspectors
c. children
d. handles

34. According to the NEC, 120-volt track lighting shall be mounted no less than _____ ft. above the finished floor except where protection from physical damage is provided.
a. 4
b. 5
c. 8
d. 10

35. NEC Section _____ covers IMC and describes its permitted uses.
a. 340.10
b. 342.10
c. 350.10
d. 410.16

36. Cables installed in electrically heated floors of bathrooms and kitchens and in hydromassage bathtub locations, shall be provide with _____ for personnel.
a. a disconnecting means
b. overcurrent protection
c. arc-fault circuit-interrupter protection
d. ground-fault circuit-interrupter protection

37. Per NEC Article _____, for ungrounded circuits, voltage to ground is defined as the greatest voltage between the given conductor and any other conductor of the circuit.
a. 100
b. 110
c. 200
d. 310

38. Which of the following NEC articles covers EMT installation requirements?
a. 90
b. 358
c. 511
d. 705

39. The door to an indoor transformer vault shall be fire rated to _____ hours.
a. 2
b. 3
c. 5
d. 12

40. What is the maximum allowable amp rating of a 125-volt Edison base fuse?
a. 10 amperes
b. 20 amperes
c. 25 amperes
d. 30 amperes

41. Receptacles above a show window shall be within _____ of the top of the window.
a. 6 inches
b. 12 inches
c. 18 inches
d. 36 inches

42. NEC Section _____ is used to determine the minimum depth of cover requirements for raceways, cables, and conductors rated for direct burial.
a. 220.42
b. 300.5
c. 300.50
d. 680.10

43. The connection between a grounded circuit conductor and an equipment grounding conductor at a separately derived system is the _____.
a. equipment bonding jumper
b. system bonding jumper
c. grounding electrode conductor
d. ground fault

44. Article _____ deals with the installation requirements for feeders and branch circuits installed outside.
a. 210
b. 215
c. 225
d. 340

45. A 12-AWG conductor requires a volume of _____ cubic inches when doing a box fill calculation.
a. 2.00
b. 2.25
c. 3.00
d. 5.00

46. Metal boxes require a minimum of _____ of the outer jacket of nonmetallic-sheathed cable inside the box and beyond the cable clamps.
a. 0 in.
b. $\frac{1}{8}$ in.
c. $\frac{1}{4}$ in.
d. None of the above

47. The NEC states that the minimum diameter for a round manhole is _____.
a. 12 in.
b. 24 in.
c. 26 in.
d. 48 in.

48. Conductors normally used to carry current shall be made of _____ unless otherwise provided in the National Electrical Code.
  a. copper
  b. aluminum
  c. copper-clad aluminum
  d. copper or aluminum

49. When installing a supplemental electrode for a metal underground water pipe electrode, electricians must consult which of the following NEC sections?
  a. 250.52(A)(1)
  b. 250.53(D)(2)
  c. 250.54
  d. All of the above

50. When installing type AC cable across the top of floor joists in an attic, where no protective guard strips are provided and no permanent stairs or ladders are installed, the installer shall keep the type AC cable at least _____ ft. from the nearest edge of the attic scuttle hole.
  a. 2
  b. 4
  c. 5
  d. 6

51. NEC Section _____ covers fluorescent ballasts that are installed indoors and require integral thermal protection.
  a. 410.6
  b. 410.7(B)(4)
  c. 410.130(E)(1)
  d. none of the above

52. The NEC's purpose appears in Section _____.
  a. Informative Annex C
  b. 90.1(A)
  c. 90.1(C)
  d. 110.1(A)

53. According to NEC Section _____, a disconnecting means serving a hermetic refrigerant motor compressor shall have an ampere rating of at least 115% of the nameplate rated-load current or branch circuit selection current, whichever is greater.
  a. 440.12(A)(1)
  b. 440.12(D)
  c. 440.12(A)(1) and 440.12(D)
  d. None of the above

54. According to NEC Section _____, regarding grounded systems, the Earth is not to be considered an effective ground-fault current path.
  a. 250.4(A)(5)
  b. 250.4(B)(4)
  c. 250.6
  d. 690.41

55. The term _____ means "acceptable to the AHJ."
  a. listed
  b. tested
  c. approved
  d. guaranteed

56. Excluding exceptions, Section _____ prohibits electricians from connecting the equipment grounding conductor or grounding electrodes to the grounded conductor at a building or structure supplied by a feeder or branch circuit.
  a. 250.24
  b. 250.30(A)(5)
  c. 250.32(B)
  d. All of the above

57. When a premise's wiring system is supplied by a grounded AC system of 1,000 volts or less at any point, the grounded conductor shall be routed with the ungrounded conductors to each service disconnecting means. The electrician should consult Section _____ for grounded conductors brought to service equipment.
a. 250.24(C)
b. 680.6(B)(2)
c. 680.6(B)(2) and 250.24(C)
d. None of the above

58. Where a feeder supplies continuous loads or any combination of continuous loads and noncontinuous loads, the minimum feeder conductor size shall have an allowable ampacity not less than the noncontinuous load plus _____ percent of the continuous load.
a. 50
b. 75
c. 100
d. 125

59. Electrode-type boilers operating at over 1,000 volts, nominal, should be supplied only from a three-phase, _____ system or from isolating transformers arranged to provide such a system.
a. four wire, solidly grounded wye
b. corner-grounded delta
c. four wire, solidly grounded wye and corner-grounded delta
d. None of the above

60. Cable wiring methods _____ be used as a means of support for other cables, raceways, or nonelectrical equipment.
a. shall not
b. shall
c. should not
d. are permitted to

61. The diameter of a compact bare 4/0 AWG conductor is _____.
a. 0.520 in.
b. 0.475 in.
c. 0.299 in.
d. 0.134 in.

62. The following equipment shall be permitted to be connected to the supply side of a service disconnect.
a. current-limiting device
b. solar photovoltaic systems
c. instrument transformers
d. all of the above

63. According to the NEC, a clothes closet is defined as a _____ room or space intended primarily for storage of garments and apparel.
a. semi-concealed
b. nonhabitable
c. habitable
d. unfinished

64. When installing a grounded conductor, those sized _____ and larger can be identified by a distinct white or gray marking at each of their termination points.
a. 4 AWG
b. 6 AWG
c. 8 AWG
d. 12 AWG

65. When installing a laundry outlet in a dwelling unit, there shall be a minimum of at least one _____ branch circuit for the laundry outlet(s) as required by Section 210.52(F).
a. 15-ampere
b. 20-ampere
c. 30-ampere
d. 15-ampere and 20-ampere

66. For raceways, cable assemblies, boxes, cabinets, and fittings that are installed above a suspended ceiling, _____ that do not provide secure support shall not be permitted as the sole support.
a. framing members
b. raceways identified as a means of support
c. support wires
d. None of the above

67. When applying 3 VA per square foot for dwelling unit general lighting loads as described in Table 220.12, the 3 VA does not apply to the following locations within the dwelling unit:
a. open porches
b. garages
c. unused or unfinished spaces not adaptable for future use
d. All of these locations

68. A dwelling unit containing two 120-volt small appliance branch circuits has a calculated load of _____ VA.
a. 1,500
b. 2,500
c. 3,000
d. 3,500

69. A hallway within a dwelling unit that is 21 feet long, without passing through any doorway, shall have at least _____ receptacle outlet(s).
a. zero
b. one
c. two
d. three

70. In accordance with Section _____, the interior of enclosures and raceways installed underground for 1,000 volts or less shall be considered a wet location.
a. 300.5(B)
b. 300.50(B)
c. 300.6(D)
d. 300.9

71. Excluding any exceptions, when installing a parallel conductor, the minimum-size conductor permitted to be installed is _____ AWG.
a. 1 AWG
b. 2 AWG
c. 1/0 AWG
d. 3/0 AWG

72. For service-entrance cable, the radius of the curve of the inner edge of any bend, during or after installation, shall not be less than _____ the diameter of the cable.
a. four times
b. five times
c. six times
d. seven times

73. Table _____ is used to determine the maximum rating or settings of motor branch-circuit short-circuit and ground-fault protective devices.
a. 430.72(B)
b. 430.62
c. 430.52
d. 430.22(E)

74. The FLC of a three-phase, 460-volt, 40-HP wound rotor-type motor is _____ amps.
a. 45
b. 52
c. 140
d. 290

75. Where fuses are installed for motor overload protection, a fuse shall be inserted in each _____ and also in the grounded conductor if the supply system is 3-wire, 3-phase AC with one conductor grounded.
a. bonding conductor
b. grounding conductor
c. fuse holder
d. ungrounded conductor

76. Branch circuits recognized by Article 210 shall be rated in accordance with the maximum permitted ampere rating of the _____.
a. connected load
b. ungrounded conductors
c. overcurrent protection device
d. utilization equipment

77. Each disconnection means shall be _____ to indicate its purpose unless located and arranged so the purpose is evident.
a. legibly marked
b. illuminated
c. labeled
d. None of the above

78. NEC Section _____ states that if a disconnection means is required to be lockable open elsewhere in the NEC, it shall be capable of being locked in the open position. This provision for locking shall remain in place with or without the lock installed.
a. 110.25
b. 422.31(B)
c. 430.102(A)
d. 430.103

79. Exposed raceways, cable trays, and other wiring methods, along with covers or enclosures of pull boxes and junction boxes and including conduit bodies in which any of the available conduit openings are used that contain PV power-source conductors, shall be marked with the wording _____.
a. HAZARD – PV WIRING ENCLOSED
b. WARNING: PHOTOVOLTAIC POWER SOURCE
c. PV POWER SOURCE ENCLOSED
d. None of the above

80. The currents generated in a photovoltaic (PV) system are considered _____.
a. unsafe
b. dangerous
c. unreliable
d. continuous

Answers and Explanations

1. The correct answer is **d**. In accordance with Section 90.2(A)(2), the NEC specifically states that industrial substations are covered by the installation guidelines of the National Electrical Code. Choices **a**, **b**, and **c** are incorrect because the use of the National Electrical Code is prohibited for use in underground mining installations as specified in what's not covered by the NEC in Section 90.2(B). (NEC 90.2(A) and (B))

2. The correct answer is **d**. The NEC requires the person making key electrical decisions in an electrical installation to be knowledgeable of his or her trade, equipment, operation, and the hazards involved with the electrical installation. There are many areas within the NEC that require supervision by someone considered to be a qualified person. Choice **a** is incorrect because while it is important for the electrical inspector to have detailed knowledge of electrical codes, he or she does not assume any responsibility for the actual installation. The NEC requires a qualified person to be in charge of the electrical installation as defined in Article 100. Choice **b** is incorrect because while it is important for the Authority Having Jurisdiction (AHJ) to have a general understanding of building code related information, he or she does not assume any responsibility for the actual electrical installation. The NEC requires a qualified person to be in charge of the electrical installation as defined in Article 100. Choice **c** is incorrect because while it is important for the job foreperson to have detailed knowledge of the construction site, he or she may or may not be knowledgeable in all things electrical in order to assume any responsibility for the actual electrical installation. (NEC 100)

3. The correct answer is **a**. For a parallel circuit containing multiple resistors of equal value, the Ohm's Law formula for finding the total resistance (RT) is: $R_T = R \div N$, where R equals the value of the resistors and N equals the total number of them. Therefore, the total resistance = 45 ohms $\div$ 3 = 15 ohms. Choices **b** and **c** are incorrect because in a parallel circuit, the total resistance is always less than the resistance of any branch. Therefore the total resistance of this circuit could not be 45 ohms or 135 ohms. Choice **d** is incorrect because in determining total resistance, as long as the value of all of the resistors is known, there is no need for additional information such as applied voltage or total current. (Ohm's Law)

4. The correct answer is **a**. To determine the current through the individual resistors in a parallel circuit, the Ohm's Law formula is as follows: $I = E \div R$. In this case, we are looking for the current through each resistor. Since the resistors are of equal value, the current through each will be equal. Thus, the current (I) through each resistor will be 90 volts $\div$ 45 ohms = 2 amperes. Choice **b** is incorrect because using the Ohm's Law formula $I = E \div R$, the applied voltage of 90 volts is divided by the individual resistor value and not the total resistance value, which would result in an answer of 6 amperes. Choice **c** is incorrect because an answer of 1,350 amperes would result in using an incorrect formula of $I = E \times R_{total}$ or 90 volts $\times$ 15 ohm's = 1,350 amperes. Choice **d** is incorrect because an answer of 4,050 amperes would result in using an incorrect formula of $I = E \times R_{indivicual\ values}$ or 90 volts $\times$ 45 ohms = 4,050 amperes. (Ohm's Law)

5. The correct answer is **c**. In accordance with the definition in NEC Section 427.2, induction heating systems use induced currents and hysteresis effects in the pipeline walls as part of their heating process. Choice **a** is incorrect because while resistance heating systems are an option for heating pipelines, they do not utilize induction as part of their heating process. Choice **b** is incorrect because while skin-effect heating systems are an option for heating pipelines, they do not utilize induction as part of their heating process. Choice **d** is incorrect because while impedance heating systems are an option for heating pipelines, they do not utilize induction as part of their heating process. (NEC 427.2)

6. The correct answer is **b**. The integrity of the conductor must be maintained throughout its travel; using insulation of a similar rating ensures this integrity. Choice **a** is incorrect because this material has not been evaluated for use on electrical systems by National Testing Laboratories, so it would not be an acceptable method. Choice **c** is incorrect because it would be nearly impossible for a nonmetallic plate to remain a viable alternative. The entire exposed conductor must be shielded from accidental contact, and using a plate would be impossible to achieve the required level of covering. Choice **d** is incorrect because in general, a vinyl tape would not offer the same insulating properties as traditional insulating materials unless listed for the use. Section 110.14(B) requires the insulation method to be equivalent to that of the conductors or identified insulating devices; normal vinyl tape would not be equivalent. (NEC 110.14(B))

7. The correct answer is **a**. Adequate illumination is required around service equipment, switchboards, switchgears, panel boards, or motor control centers installed indoors to ensure safe operation. Choice **b** is incorrect because Section 210.70(A)(1) addresses the lighting outlet requirements in dwelling units and does not relate to the illumination requirements specified in the question. Choice **c** is incorrect because Section 408.16 addresses damp and wet locations where switchboards and switchgear may be located and does not relate to illumination requirements. Choice **d** is incorrect because Section 410.16 addresses luminaires in clothes closets and has nothing to do with the illumination requirements around specific electrical equipment. (NEC 110.26(D))

8. The correct answer is **d**. As stated in Section 490.36, the frames of switchgear and control assemblies shall be connected to an equipment grounding conductor or, where permitted, the grounded conductor. Choice **a** is incorrect because current-limiting devices are designed to limit the amount of current in a circuit during an overload, short-circuit, or ground fault event. Choice **b** is incorrect because a nonmetallic base could be anything and is too vague to answer the question. Choice **c** is incorrect because an insulating material could be anything and is too vague to answer the question. (NEC 490.36)

9. The correct answer is **b**. In accordance with the warning notice in Section 647.7(2), lighting equipment is prohibited from being connected to receptacles. The reason for these requirements is to make as certain as possible that the receptacles aren't used for cord- and plug-connected loads like lamps when supplied by the types of separately derived systems used within the scope of this article. Choice **a** is incorrect because Article 647 does not reference motors when working with sensitive electronic equipment. Choice **c** is incorrect because Article 647 does not reference telecom equipment when working with sensitive electronic equipment. Choice **d** is incorrect because Article 647 does not reference computers when working with sensitive electronic equipment. (NEC 647.7(A)(2))

10. The correct answer is **c**. Article 725 addresses the requirements for Class 1, 2, and 3 remote control and signaling. Choice **a** is incorrect because Article 330 addresses metal-clad cable and has nothing to do with Class 1, 2, and 3 circuits. Choice **b** is incorrect because Article 525 addresses carnivals, circuses, fairs, and similar events and has nothing to do with Class 1, 2, and 3 circuits. Choice **d** is incorrect because Article 730 does not exist in the NEC. (NEC 725).

11. The correct answer is **b**. Up to 18 in. above the floor, an aircraft hangar, including its associated areas, is considered a Class 1, Division 2 or Zone 2 location. Choices **b** and **d** are incorrect because in accordance with the National Electrical Code, the specific area of a hangar, including any adjacent and communication areas not suitably cut off from the hangar, are classified as Class 1, Division 2 or Zone 2 from the floor up to a level of 18 in. (NEC 513.3(B))

12. The correct answer is **b**. As defined in 680.2, a forming shell is a structural element designed to install wet-niche luminaires in pools and fountains. Choice **a** is incorrect because nothing within Article 680 references the term *wet mount*. The actual structure to which a wet niche is mounted is called a forming shell. Choice **c** is incorrect because nothing within Article 680 references the term *moisture barrier* in terms of a structural mounting component. Choice **d** is incorrect because nothing within Article 680 references the term *moisture shunt* in terms of a structural mounting component. The actual structure to which a wet niche is mounted is called a forming shell. (NEC 680.2)

13. The correct answer is **c**. According to the informational note, guidance is given in Section 500.6(A)(2), in which hydrogen is used as an example of a Class 1, Group B material. The class is based on it being in ignitable concentrations, and the group is based on its flammability and explosive pressures as expressed in Section 500.6(A). Choice **a** is incorrect because Group A is for acetylene only. Choice **b** is incorrect because Class 2 is for combustible dust. Choice **d** is incorrect because Class 2 is for combustible dust. (NEC 500.6(A)(2))

14. The correct answer is **b**. Article 770 addresses the use of optical fiber cables and raceways. Choice **a** is incorrect because Article 600 addresses electric signs and outline lighting, not optical fiber cables. Choice **c** is incorrect because Article 800 addresses communication circuits and not optical fiber cables and raceways. Choice **d** is incorrect because Article 821 does not exist within the NEC. (NEC 770)

15. The correct answer is **b**. Class 1 circuits are either power limited or protected by an overcurrent device at their source. When using the option where overcurrent protection is protecting the conductors, the voltage is limited to 600 volts, as specified in NEC 725.41(B). Choice **a** is incorrect because 1,000 volts exceeds the express demand by the NEC in section 725.41(B) to not exceed 600 volts. Choice **c** is incorrect because although 150 volts is not a problem, it is not the best answer to the question, which asks for a maximum value that the circuit can't exceed. 150 volts is too low and impracticable. Choice **d** is incorrect because although 30 volts is not a problem, it is not the best answer for the question, which asks for a maximum value that the circuit can't exceed. 30 volts is too low and impracticable. (NEC 725)

16. The correct answer is **c**. When it comes to outlet boxes that are specifically designed for supporting suspended ceiling fans, they need be marked in order to confirm the evaluated supporting thresholds of the manufacturer. If they are listed specifically for the fan support, then it is assumed that it can handle a fan of 35 lbs., but anything over that needs to ensure its design will accommodate the increased weight. Choice **a** is incorrect because while 75 lbs. would technically be acceptable, the question is looking for the threshold to which a listed outlet box designed to support a ceiling-suspended paddle fan has to exceed in order to require actual markings on the listed outlet box. Choice **b** is incorrect because while 50 lbs. would technically be acceptable, the question is looking for the threshold to which a listed outlet box designed to support a ceiling-suspended paddle fan has to exceed in order to require actual markings on the listed outlet box. Choice **d** is incorrect because a weight of 25 lbs. would be insufficient, as the markings are not required on the listed outlet box designed for a suspended ceiling fan of 35 lbs. or less, and the question is looking for the threshold to which a listed outlet box designed to support a ceiling-suspended paddle fan has to exceed in order to require actual markings on the listed outlet box. (NEC 314.27(C))

17. The correct answer is **c**. While the NEC does permit receptacle outlets above, in, or, in special circumstances, below the work surface, the question focuses on them being located above the work surface. Choices **a** and **b** are incorrect because these would be less than the maximum of 20 in., but the question calls for the maximum height above the work surface that the installer is not permitted to exceed. Choice **d** is incorrect because this would exceed the maximum permitted of 20 in. (NEC 210.52(C)(5))

18. The correct answer is **c**. A drinking fountain is not considered a fountain according to the National Electrical Code. Choice **a** is incorrect because a reflecting pool is indeed a fountain according to the definition of a fountain in Section 680.2. Choice **b** is incorrect because a display pool is indeed a fountain according to the definition of fountain in Section 680.2. Choice **d** is incorrect because a drinking fountain is not considered a fountain, as stated in Section 680.2. (NEC 680.2)

19. The correct answer is **d**. All of these statements about effective grounding paths are true. Choices **a**, **b**, and **c** are incorrect because while they are each true statements, the other statements are also true. (NEC 250.68(B))

20. The correct answer is **a**. The branch circuit conductors supplying one or more units of information technology equipment shall have an ampacity of not less than 125% of the total connected load. Choice **b** is incorrect because the question asks for a value *not less than*; 150% incorrectly matches the hard value given in the NEC. Choice **c** is incorrect because the question asks for a value *not less than*; 175% incorrectly matches the hard value given in the NEC. Choice **d** is incorrect because 150% would be excessive, as the question asks for a value *not less than*; choosing 200% incorrectly matches the hard value given in the NEC. (NEC 645.5(A))

21. The correct answer is **b**. NEC 410.116(A)(1) specifies that a recessed luminaire not identified for contact with insulation must be no less than $\frac{1}{2}$ inch away from combustible materials. Choice **a** is incorrect because this answer is less than the minimum separation value of $\frac{1}{2}$ inch. Choice **c** is incorrect because while it is correct that $\frac{3}{4}$ inch is more than the minimum of the $\frac{1}{2}$-inch separation, the question asks for the minimum value and this answer exceeds that minimum value. Choice **d** is incorrect because while it is correct that 1 inch is more than the minimum of the $\frac{1}{2}$-inch separation, the question asks for the minimum value and this answer exceeds that minimum value. (NEC 410.116(A)(1))

22. The correct answer is **a**. While Article 342 provides details on IMC and the minimum and maximum trade sizes permitted, it does not actually give the entire scope of trade sizes and their metric equivalent. Section 300.1(C) provides a detailed reference to all sizes of conduit, tubing, and associated fittings. The correct answer is 27. (NEC 300.1(C))

23. The correct answer is **a**. $\frac{1}{2}$-in. trade size of ENT has a nominal internal diameter of 0.602 in., as defined in Table 4 of Chapter 9 in the NEC. Choice **b** is incorrect because the value shown in this answer (0.804) would be for $\frac{3}{4}$-inch trade size of ENT. Choice **c** is incorrect because the value shown in this answer (1.029) would be for 1-inch trade size of ENT. Choice **d** is incorrect because the value shown in this answer (2.047) would be for 2-in. trade size of ENT. (NEC Chapter 9, Table 4)

24. The correct answer is **d**. Based on Table 310.15(B)(16), the allowable ampacity of a 10 AWG CU is 40 amperes. Keep in mind that Section 240.4(D)(7) will limit the current to 30 amperes for overcurrent protection. However, based on the definition of *ampacity*, the starting value, before any adjustments or corrections to a THHN conductor, is in the 90 degrees Celsius column. Choices **a**, **b**, and **c** are incorrect. (NEC Table 310.15(B)(16))

25. The correct answer is **a**. Air conditioners and equipment with hermetic refrigeration are covered within NEC Article 440. Choice **b** is incorrect because Article 450 addresses transformers. Choice **c** is incorrect because Article 610 addresses cranes and hoists. Choice **d** is incorrect because Article 625 addresses electric vehicles. (NEC 440)

26. The correct answer is **b**. Table 210.24 provides a summary of the branch circuit requirements. Choice **a** is incorrect because this table provides receptacle ratings for various sizes of circuits but does not refer to any summary of branch circuits. Choice **c** is incorrect because Table 220.42 is used to calculate the lighting load demand factors for a service or feeder calculation and is not germane to the question. Choice **d** is incorrect because this table provides depth of cover requirements for network-power broadband cable systems and has nothing to do with branch circuits. (NEC 210.24)

27. The correct answer is **c**. A continuous-duty power-resistor conductor must be rated at 110% of full-load current. Choice **a** is incorrect because power-resistor conductors used with a continuous-duty motor are required to be rated no less than 110% of the FLC. The value of 60% would be less than the stated code mandate. Choice **b** is incorrect because the value of 80% would be less than the stated code mandate. Choice **d** is incorrect because the value of 120% would exceed the stated code mandate. While it would not be a code violation to exceed the minimum of 110% of the FLC, it would result in higher cost of material and would not meet the minimum rating as requested within the question. (NEC 430.29, Table 430.29)

28. The correct answer is **c**. Type USE is rated for 75°C as stated in Section 310.104(A). However, if you see USE-2, the -2 denotes that it is rated for 90°C. The normal USE is not rated for 90°C. Choices **a**, **b**, and **d** are incorrect because these types of insulation are rated for 90°C in a dry or wet location. (NEC 310.104(A))

29. The correct answer is **b**. Electrical metallic tubing can be installed, concealed, or exposed. Choice **a** is incorrect because electrical metallic tubing does not provide protection against severe physical damage, as its thin wall is not designed for that. Choice **c** is incorrect because electrical metallic tubing cannot be used for luminaire support, as is specifically stated in Section 358.12(5). Choice **d** is incorrect because where practicable, electrical metallic tubing shall avoid contact with dissimilar metals to avoid the potential for galvanic action, as is specifically stated in Section 358.12(5). (NEC 358.12)

30. The correct answer is **d**. Per NEC Section 215.2(B)(1), electricians who are calculating transformer feeder ampacity should use the transformer's nameplate ratings. Choice **a** is incorrect because Article 705 addresses interconnected electrical power production sources and does not relate to transformers or feeders. Choice **b** is incorrect because Article 554 doesn't exist within the National Electrical Code. Choice **c** is incorrect because Section 450.5(A)(4) addresses ratings of autotransformers and neutral-current values that are not to be rated less than the specified ground-fault current. (NEC 215.2(B)(1))

31. The correct answer is **b**. Electricians installing more than 3 current-carrying conductors in a raceway or cable should consult NEC Section 310.15(B)(3)(a), which will reference Table 310.15(B)(3)(a) for a percentage value to be applied to adjust the ampacity of a conductor based on condition of use. Choice **a** is incorrect because this answer deals with a correction factor for an elevated ambient temperature for conductors outside of the scope of temperatures given in Table 310.15(B)(16), which will need to be taken into account when installing conductors in cables and raceways where the ambient temperatures are other than 30°C. The answer is NEC 310.15(B)(3)(a), which covers the adjustment for more than 3 current-carrying conductors in a cable or raceway. Choice **c** is incorrect because this section is specific to dwelling units with single-phase applications that are limited to 120-/240-volt applications. Choice **d** is incorrect. (NEC 310.15(B)(3)(a))

32. The correct answer is **b**. The manufacturer will mark ENT every 10 ft., and the marking will include all the information demanded by Section 110.21(A). Choice **a** is incorrect because marking every 12 ft. could not be compliant with the NEC. Choices **c** and **d** are incorrect because the manufacturers could provide markings less than 10 ft., but this would increase the cost of the product and is not typically done. (NEC 362.120)

33. The correct answer is **a**. It is very important to install knife switch-type disconnects in a manner that will not allow gravity to close them and accidentally energize the circuit while it is intended to be de-energized. While you want the inspector to find the equipment; this answer does not relate specifically to the knife switch. The NEC is not specifically driven for children in general. The NEC is a minimum safety document to protect everyone from the risks of working with electricity. While handles may appear to work, many knife switches do not have handles. In addition, this answer does not relate to the question at hand. (NEC 404.6(A))

34. The correct answer is **b**. Section 410.151(C)(8) is very specific regarding the minimum acceptable height of track lighting, and anything less than the minimums would be a direct violation of the NEC. Choice **a** is incorrect because anything less than the minimums would be a direct violation of the NEC. Choices **c** and **d** are incorrect because anything more than the minimums would be technically acceptable but is not the focus of this question. (NEC 410.151(C)(8))

35. The correct answer is **b**. NEC Article 342 covers IMC and describes its permitted uses. Choice **a** is incorrect because Article 340 addresses underground feeder cables used for branch and feeder circuits. Choice **c** is incorrect because Article 350 addresses the permitted uses of liquid-tight flexible metal conduits and not IMC. Choice **d** is incorrect because NEC Article 342 covers IMC and describes its permitted uses. Article 410 addresses luminaires and does not relate to wiring methods or IMC. (NEC 342.10)

36. The correct answer is **d**. Ground-fault circuit-interrupter protection is required for personnel in electrically heated floors. Choice **a** is incorrect because while a disconnecting means must be provided for all circuits installed in accordance with the NEC, they are not provided for the protection of personnel in electrically heated floors. Choice **b** is incorrect because while an overcurrent protection must be provided for all circuits installed in accordance with the NEC, it is not provided for the protection of personnel in electrically heated floors. Choice **c** is incorrect because arc-fault circuit-interrupter protection is not required for personnel in electrically heated floors. (NEC 424.44(E))

37. The correct answer is **a**. Per NEC Article 100, for ungrounded circuits, voltage to ground is defined as the greatest voltage between the given conductor and any other conductor of the circuit. Choice **b** is incorrect because Article 110 addresses the requirements for electrical installations and will not provide the definition of a "voltage to ground." Choice **c** is incorrect because Article 200 addresses the uses and identification of grounded conductors and will not provide the definition of a "voltage to ground." Choice **d** is incorrect because Article 310 addresses conductors for general wiring and will not provide the definition of a "voltage to ground." (NEC 100)

38. The correct answer is **b**. NEC Article 358 identifies EMT installation requirements. Choice **a** is incorrect because this article addresses the introductory information for the National Electrical Code. It does not contain any information regarding Article 358 and EMT. Choice **c** is incorrect because this article addresses commercial garages, repair, and storage facilities, and while EMT is a permitted wiring method within these various locations, Article 511 does not address electrical metallic tubing. Choice **d** is incorrect because this article addresses interconnected electric power production sources, and while EMT is a permitted wiring method used with interconnected systems like PV and wind generation systems, Article 705 does not address electrical metallic tubing. (NEC 358)

39. The correct answer is **b**. The door to an indoor transformer vault shall be fire rated to 3 hours to maintain the same rating of the walls, floors, and ceilings. Choice **a** is incorrect because having a door rating of 2 hours would be the weakest link of the vault ratings since walls, floors, and ceilings, excluding exceptions, are rated for 3 hours. The doors to the indoor vault shall be 3-hour rated and tight fitting. Choice **c** is incorrect because the door to an indoor transformer vault shall be fire rated to 3 hours to maintain the same rating of the walls, floors, and ceilings. Having a door that is rated 5 hours would be excessive considering the walls, floors, and ceilings are only rated 3 hours. Choice **d** is incorrect because having a door that is rated 12 hours would be excessive considering the walls, floors, and ceilings are only rated 3 hours. (NEC 450.43(A))

40. The correct answer is **d**. The upper limit for Edison fuses is 30 amperes per Section 240.51 of the National Electrical Code. Choice **a** is incorrect because, based on 240.6(A), 10-ampere fuses are considered standard. However, they are not the maximum allowable ampere-rated 125-volt Edison base fuses available in the selection of answers. Choice **b** is incorrect because, based on 240.6(A), 20-ampere fuses are considered standard. However, they are not the maximum allowable ampere-rated 125-volt Edison base fuses available in the selection of answers. Choice **c** is incorrect because, based on 240.6(A), 25-ampere fuses are considered standard. However, they are not the maximum allowable ampere-rated 125-volt Edison base fuses available in the selection of answers. (NEC 240.51)

41. The correct answer is **c**. At least one 125-volt, single-phase, 15- or 20-ampere-rated receptacle shall be installed within 18 inches of the top of the show window for each 12 linear feet or major faction. Choice **a** is incorrect because while the NEC does say within 18 inches, and 6 inches would be a code-compliant installation, the question is asking for the maximum distance from the show window that the receptacle must be located, and 18 inches is the threshold. Choice **b** is incorrect because while 12 inches would be a code-compliant installation, the question is asking for the maximum distance from the show window that the receptacle must be located, and 18 inches is the threshold. Choice **d** is incorrect because 36 inches would be beyond the maximum distance of 18 inches, thereby resulting in an NEC violation. (NEC 210.62)

42. The correct answer is **b**. Depending on the conduit, tubing, cable, and direct burial cable the electrician uses for an underground installation, the burial depth as well as Section 300.5 and Table 300.5 determine associated depth of cover to the finished grade. Choice **a** is incorrect because Section 220.42 is used for service and feeder calculations. Choice **c** is incorrect because Section 300.50 is similar to 300.5, but it is used on systems over 1,000 volts. Choice **d** is incorrect because Table 300.5 determines associated depth of cover to the finished grade. (NEC 300.5, Table 300.5)

43. The correct answer is **b**. The connection between a grounded circuit conductor and the supply-side bonding jumper or the equipment grounding conductor, or both at a separately derived system, is the system bonding jumper. Choice **a** is incorrect because an equipment bonding jumper is used to connect two or more portions of the equipment grounding conductors. It is not used between the equipment grounding conductor and a separately derived system. Choice **c** is incorrect because a grounding electrode conductor is used to connect the electrical system's grounded conductor or the equipment to a grounding electrode or to a point on the grounding electrode system. Choice **d** is incorrect because a ground fault is an unintentional contact between an ungrounded conductor (hot) and what would normally be non–current-carrying conductors, metallic enclosures, metallic raceways, metallic equipment, or Earth. The other options are actual conductors serving a purpose, but a ground fault is due to an unforeseen or unintended condition. (NEC 100)

44. The correct answer is **c**. Article 225 covers the requirements for outside branch circuits and feeders run on or between buildings, structures, or poles on the premises along with associated electrical equipment located on or attached to the outside of those structures. Choice **a** is incorrect because Article 210 addresses branch circuits only and not feeders or outside conditions. Choice **b** is incorrect because Article 215 does cover feeders but not the location of feeders outside along with branch circuit conductors. Choice **d** is incorrect because Article 340 addresses an actual wiring method. While type UF cable can be used for both feeders and branch circuits, the question refers to the installation requirements for feeders and branch circuits located outside, which Article 225 addresses. (NEC 225)

45. The correct answer is **b**. According to Table 314.16(B), the volume allowance for a 12-AWG conductor is 2.25 cubic inches. Choice **a** is incorrect because the value 2.00 would be for a 14-AWG conductor. Choice **c** is incorrect because the value 3.0 would be for an 8-AWG conductor. Choice **d** is incorrect because the value 5.00 would be for a 6-AWG conductor. (NEC 314.16(B))

46. The correct answer is **c**. When installing type NM cable into a connector, the installer has to ensure that no less than $\frac{1}{4}$ in. of the sheathing extends into the box and beyond the cable clamp. This ensures that the cable will not pull out of the connector and expose the individual conductors to the sharp edges of the cable clamp. Choice **b** is incorrect because the $\frac{1}{8}$ in. depicted in this answer would be less than the minimum of $\frac{1}{4}$ in. Choices **a** and **d** are also incorrect.

47. The correct answer is **c**. The NEC requires that a round manhole be no less than 26 inches in diameter. Choice **b** is incorrect because the purpose of a manhole is to allow entry for working on electrical systems that require access to a degree that a handhole can't accommodate. Having a 12-in. manhole would not permit anyone to access without much discomfort. Choice **b** is incorrect because the NEC requires that a round manhole be no less than 26 inches in diameter. Choice **d** is incorrect because while it is possible to have a manhole of this size, it is not practical. The question asks for the minimum diameter because there is no technical maximum. (NEC 110.75(A))

48. The correct answer is **d**. According to the NEC, current-carrying conductors shall be made of copper or aluminum unless permitted elsewhere in the NEC. Choices **a**, **b**, and **c** are incorrect. (NEC 110.5)

49. The correct answer is **b**. When an underground water pipe grounding electrode qualifies per Section 250.52(A)(1), it is required to have a supplemental electrode as described in Section 250.53(D)(2). Choice **a** is incorrect because 250.52(A)(1) provides a description of an underground water pipe grounding electrode. The question is asking about the required supplemental electrodes. Choice **c** is incorrect because 250.54 describes the requirements for an auxiliary electrode, which is not a supplemental electrode. Choice **d** is incorrect because the question is asking about the required supplemental electrodes, which can be found in Section 250.53(D)(2). (NEC 250.53(D)(2))

50. The correct answer is **d**. In attics where guard strips do not provide protection and there is no permanent access to the attic by stairs or ladders, type AC cable shall be installed at least 6 ft. from the nearest edge of the scuttle hole or guard strips must be added to protect the cables. Choices **a**, **b**, and **c** are incorrect because the minimum clearance without protection is 6 ft. (NEC 250.53(D)(2))

51. The correct answer is **c**. The ballasts of a fluorescent luminaire installed indoors shall have integral thermal protection. This also applies to replacement ballasts. Choice **a** is incorrect because 410.6 expresses that all luminaires are to be listed, which does not address the question. The ballasts of a fluorescent luminaire installed indoors shall have integral thermal protection. This also applies to replacement ballasts. Choice **b** is incorrect because this section does not exist within the National Electrical Code. The ballasts of a fluorescent luminaire installed indoors shall have integral thermal protection. This also applies to replacement ballasts. Choice **d** is incorrect because 410.130(E)(1) states that the ballasts of a fluorescent luminaire installed indoors shall have integral thermal protection. This also applies to replacement ballasts. (NEC 410.130(E)(1))

52. The correct answer is **b**. The NEC's purpose is to provide a practical safeguard of persons and property from hazards arising from the use of electricity. Choice **a** is incorrect because informative annexes are informational only and do not provide code requirements. Choice **c** is incorrect because Section 90.1(C) addresses other equivalent international standards that are contained in Section 131 of the International Electrotechnical Commission Standards. Choice **d** is incorrect because this section does not exist in the NEC. While 110.1 does present the scope of that Article, Requirements for Electrical Installations, it has nothing to do with the purpose of the NEC. (NEC 90.1(A))

53. The correct answer is **a**. NEC 440.12(A)(1) addresses the need for the disconnection means for a hermetic refrigerant motor compressor to have an ampere rating of at least 115% of the nameplate rating or otherwise as expressed. Choice **b** is incorrect because it simply points the installer to comply with Section 440.12. NEC 440.12(A)(1) addresses the need for the disconnection means for a hermetic refrigerant motor compressor to have an ampere rating of at least 115% of the nameplate rating or otherwise as expressed. Choice **c** is incorrect because while 440.12(A)(1) is correct, 440.12(D) is incorrect and simply points the installer to comply with Section 440.12. NEC 440.12(A)(1) addresses the need for the disconnection means for a hermetic refrigerant motor compressor to have an ampere rating of at least 115% of the nameplate rating or otherwise as expressed. Choice **d** is incorrect because NEC 440.12(A)(1) addresses the need for the disconnection means for a hermetic refrigerant motor compressor to have an ampere rating of at least 115% of the nameplate rating or otherwise as expressed. (NEC 440.12(A)(1))

54. The correct answer is **a**. As stated in the last sentence of Section 250.4(A)(5), the Earth is never to be considered an effective ground-fault current path. While current does travel on the Earth under certain conditions, it does not present a low enough impedance path to facilitate the proper operation of overcurrent protective devices and shall not be relied upon. Choice **b** is incorrect because while this statement is contained within Section 250.4(B)(4), it addresses ungrounded systems and this question is asking specifically about grounded systems. Choice **c** is incorrect because this code section is referring to objectionable currents and does not provide information regarding the Earth being used as an effective ground-fault current path. Choice **d** is incorrect because this section references the grounding requirements for a photovoltaic system and does not address the question being asked. (NEC 690.41)

55. The correct answer is **c**. The authority having jurisdiction (AHJ) has the final approval powers on all installations. While they are to use the NEC as a technical standard, there are many locations within the NEC that require the AHJ to make the final call on technical equivalency. Choice **a** is incorrect because listings are used to help the AHJ make an approval, but listings are specifically on electrical products and not on the AHJ's acceptance authority. Choice **b** is incorrect because testing is something that the manufacturers do prior to being listed and evaluated. While the AHJ can require some field testing, it is not a stand-alone basis for acceptance. Choice **d** is incorrect because the AHJ will never guarantee anything as inspections are simply snapshots in time, and as such, they can't control what happens after the project is completed. (NEC 100)

56. The correct answer is **c**. In order to eliminate the issue of objectionable currents and energizing components in the electrical system that are not normally energized, the NEC attempts to reduce the risk of circulating currents by directing the installer to not make improper case to neutral connections downstream of the service disconnect. Choice **a** is incorrect because this section addresses the requirement to bring a grounded conductor to the service disconnection means. It does not address the issue in the question. Choice **b** is incorrect because this section is for grounding electrode conductors for a single separately derived system and does not relate to the question being asked. Choice **d** is incorrect because the correct answer is 250.32(B). In order to eliminate the issue of objectionable currents and energizing components in the electrical system that are not normally energized, the NEC attempts to reduce the risk of circulating currents by directing the installer to not make improper case to neutral connections downstream of the service disconnect. (NEC 250.32(B))

57. The correct answer is **a**. Remember that in a grounded system, electricity flows on a closed loop from the source to the load and back to the source. Bringing a grounded conductor to the service disconnecting means provides a return current path for the system. Choice **b** is incorrect because this section does not exist. Also, Article 680 addresses swimming pools, fountains, and similar installations. Choice **c** is incorrect because 680.6(B)(2) does not exist. Also, Article 680 addresses swimming pools, fountains, and similar installations. Choice **d** is incorrect because the correct answer is 250.24(C). (NEC 250.24(C))

58. The correct answer is **d**. Continuous loads are defined as a load where the maximum current is expected to continue for 3 hours or more. The NEC also specifies certain loads as continuous loads. Choice **a** is incorrect because the NEC demands that 100% of the noncontinuous loads and 125% of the continuous loads be considered. 50% would not be adequate to meet the load calculations for the feeder. Continuous loads are defined in Article 100. Choice **b** is incorrect because 75% would not be adequate to meet the load calculations for the feeder. Continuous loads are defined in Article 100. Choice **c** is incorrect because the noncontinuous load is at 100%, but the continuous loads that are expected to have a maximum current draw for 3 hours or more are at 125%. (NEC 215.2(A)(1)(a)

59. The correct answer is **a**. Electrode-type boilers operating at over 1,000 volts, nominal, should be supplied only from a three-phase, four-wire, solidly grounded wye system or from isolating transformers arranged to provide such a system. Choice **b** is incorrect because the requirement clearly only applies to a three-phase, four-wire, solidly grounded system. A corner-grounded system would not apply. Choice **c** is incorrect because the requirement only applies to a three-phase, four-wire, solidly grounded system. It would not apply to a corner-grounded system. Choice **d** is incorrect because Electrode-type boilers operating at over 1,000 volts, nominal, should be supplied only from a three-phase, four-wire, solidly grounded wye system or from isolating transformers arranged to provide such a system. (NEC 490.71)

60. The correct answer is **a**. Cable wiring methods shall not be used as a means of support for other cables, raceways, or nonelectrical equipment as stated in Section 300.11(D). Choice **b** is incorrect because the term *shall* is a mandatory rule, and the NEC says *shall not* in the case of using a cable to support other cables, raceways, or nonelectrical equipment. Choice **c** is incorrect because cable wiring methods *shall not* be used as a means of support for other cables, raceways, or nonelectrical equipment as stated in Section 300.11(D). The phrase *should not* is subjective and is not in accordance with the NEC Manual of Style. Choice **d** is incorrect because cable wiring methods *shall not* be used as a means of support for other cables, raceways, or nonelectrical equipment as stated in Section 300.11(D). The phrase *are permitted to* is subjective and is not in accordance with the NEC Manual of Style. (NEC 300.11(D))

61. The correct answer is **b**. According to NEC Table 5A, the diameter of a compact bare 4/0-AWG conductor is 0.475 in. Choice **a** is incorrect because the 0.520 in. given in this answer is for a 500-kcmil conductor. Choice **c** is incorrect because the 0.299 in. given in this answer is for a 1-AWG conductor. Choice **d** is incorrect because the 0.134 in. given in this answer is for a 8-AWG conductor. (NEC Chapter 9, Table 5A)

62. The correct answer is **d**. All of the items in this list of answers are permitted to be placed ahead of the service disconnection means in accordance with Section 230.82. Choice **a** is incorrect because while current-limiting devices are permitted to be connected on the supply side of a service disconnect, the question asks which of the items listed are permitted for this application as defined in Section 230.82. All of the electrical equipment is permitted for connection ahead of the service disconnection means. Choice **b** is incorrect because while a solar photovoltaic is permitted to be connected on the supply side of a service disconnect, the question asks which of the items listed are permitted for this application as defined in Section 230.82. All of the electrical equipment is permitted for connection ahead of the service disconnection means. Choice **c** is incorrect because while instrument transformers are permitted to be connected on the supply side of a service disconnect, the question asks which of the items listed are permitted for this application as defined in Section 230.82. All of the electrical equipment is permitted for connection ahead of the service disconnection means. (NEC 230.82)

63. The correct answer is **b**. The NEC defines a clothes closet as a nonhabitable room or space. Choice **a** is incorrect because a space is either concealed or exposed, and neither would apply to a clothes closet. The NEC defines a clothes closet as a nonhabitable room or space. Choice **c** is incorrect because the NEC defines a clothes closet as a nonhabitable room or space. Choice **d** is incorrect because finished or unfinished does not relate to the definition of a clothes closet. (NEC 100)

64. The correct answer is **a**. According to Section 200.6(B)(4), a conductor 4 AWG and larger, at the time of the installation, can be identified by a distinct white or gray marking at each of their termination points. Choice **b** is incorrect because 6 AWG is too small to meet this requirement. Choice **c** is incorrect because 8 AWG is too small to meet this requirement. Choice **d** is incorrect because 12 AWG is too small to meet this requirement. According to Section 200.6(B)(4), a conductor 4 AWG and larger, at the time of the installation, can be identified by a distinct white or gray marking at each of their termination points rather than being continuous white, gray, or any color other than green, with three continuous white or gray stripes. (NEC 200.6(B)(4))

65. The correct answer is **b**. Section 210.11(C)(2) mandates at least one 20-amp circuit to supply the laundry outlets mandated by Section 210.52(F). Choice **a** is incorrect because while nothing in the NEC would prohibit the installation of a 15A branch circuit in the laundry area, it would not meet the requirement for at least one 20A branch circuit for the outlets described in Section 210.52(F). Section 210.11(C)(2) mandates at least one 20-amp circuit to supply the laundry outlets mandated by Section 210.52(F). Also, the NEC does not require a 30A dryer circuit or outlet. Choice **c** is incorrect because while nothing in the NEC would prohibit the installation of a 30A branch circuit in the laundry area, it would not meet the requirement for at least one 20A branch circuit for the outlets described in Section 210.52(F). Section 210.11(C)(2) mandates at least one 20-amp branch circuit to supply the laundry outlets mandated by Section 210.52(F). Also, the NEC does not require a 30A dryer circuit or outlet. Choice **d** is incorrect because while nothing in the NEC would prohibit the installation of a 15A branch circuit in the laundry area, it would not meet the requirement for at least one 20A branch circuit for the outlets described in Section 210.52(F). Section 210.11(C)(2) mandates at least one 20-amp circuit to supply the laundry outlets mandated by Section 210.52(F). Also, the NEC does not require a 30A dryer circuit or outlet. (NEC 210.11(C)(2))

66. The correct answer is **c**. Above suspended ceilings, support wires that do not provide secure support shall not be permitted as the sole support of raceways, cable assemblies, boxes, cabinets, and fittings. Choice **a** is incorrect because a framing member located above a suspended ceiling would provide adequate support for raceways, cable assemblies, boxes, cabinets, and fittings. Choice **b** is incorrect because Section 300.11(C)(1) states that raceways that are identified as a means of support may be used as such. Choice **d** is incorrect because above suspended ceilings, support wires that do not provide secure support shall not be permitted as the sole support of raceways, cable assemblies, boxes, cabinets, and fittings. (NEC 300.11(B))

67. The correct answer is **d**. Open porches, garages, and unused or unfinished spaces not adaptable for future use are all to be excluded in the 3 VA per square foot calculation given in Table 220.12. Choice **a** is incorrect because while open porches is on the list of items in Section 220.12 to be excluded, there are other locations listed that are to be excluded from the square footage calculation. All of the locations given are correct. Choice **b** is incorrect because while garages is on the list of items in Section 220.12 to be excluded, there are other locations listed that are to be excluded from the square footage calculation. All of the locations given are correct. Choice **c** is incorrect because while unused or unfinished spaces not adaptable for future use is on the list of items in Section 220.12 to be excluded, there are other locations listed that are to be excluded from the square footage calculation. All of the locations given are correct. (NEC 220.12)

68. The correct answer is **c**. In accordance with Section 220.52(A), each small appliance branch circuit has a calculated load of 1,500 volt-amperes. Since two small appliance branch circuits were given in the question, the total VA shall be 1,500 × 2, resulting in 3,000 VA. Choice **a** is incorrect because two small appliance branch circuits were given in the question—the total VA shall be 1,500 × 2, resulting in 3,000 VA, not 1,500 VA. Choice **b** is incorrect because two small appliance branch circuits were given in the question, the total VA shall be 1,500 × 2, resulting in 3,000 VA, not 2,500 VA. Choice **d** is incorrect because two small appliance branch circuits were given in the question, the total VA shall be 1,500 × 2, resulting in 3,000 VA, not 3,500 VA. (NEC 220.52(A))

69. The correct answer is **b**. The NEC states that any hallway at least 10 ft. or more in length shall have at least one receptacle outlet. If the hallway depicted in the question had a doorway that divided the hallway into one 10-ft. and one 11-ft. hallway, then both portions would have a minimum of one receptacle outlet each. Choice **a** is incorrect because any hallway 10 ft. or more in length must have at least one receptacle outlet. If the hallway had a doorway that divided the spaces into one 10-ft. and one 11-ft. hallway, then both portions would have a minimum of one receptacle outlet each. Choices **c** and **d** are incorrect because while you can have as many receptacle outlets as you wish in a hallway, the NEC says that any hallway at least 10 ft. or more in length shall have at least one receptacle outlet. If the hallway had a doorway that divided the spaces into one 10-ft. and one 11-ft. hallway, then both portions would have a minimum of one receptacle outlet each. (NEC 210.52(H))

70. The correct answer is **a**. Regardless of the raceway being used, if it is installed underground, the interior of the raceway is considered to be a wet location and will require conductors that are rated for the wet location environment. Choice **b** is incorrect because this reference is for over 1,000-volt applications. Regardless of the raceway or voltage applied being used, if it is installed underground, the interior of the raceway is considered to be a wet location and will require conductors that are rated for the wet location environment. Choice **c** is incorrect because this reference is for wet locations indoors and provides guidance for maintaining air spacing between the raceway and the mounting surface depending on the material to which the raceway is being secured. However, it does not directly relate to the question, so it is not the best possible answer. Choice **d** is incorrect because the reference to Section 300.9 is for raceways in wet locations above ground. The interiors of these raceways are considered wet locations as well, but the question asked for underground locations. (NEC 300.5(B))

71. The correct answer is **c**. While there are some exceptions to the general rule that would permit parallel conductors smaller than 1/0 AWG, the question did not consider any of the exceptions. Choice **a** is incorrect because 1 AWG is too small of a conductor to meet the minimum conductor size for parallels in accordance with Section 300.10(H). Choice **b** is incorrect because 2 AWG is too small of a conductor to meet the minimum conductor size for parallels in accordance with Section 300.10(H). Choice **d** is incorrect because while 3/0 AWG is larger than 1/0 AWG and would be acceptable per the NEC to be installed in parallel installations, the question asks for the minimum size permitted. (NEC 310.10(H)(1))

72. The correct answer is **b**. Bending a cable too tightly can damage not only the cable sheathing but also the conductors inside the cable. When the NEC specifies a minimum radius bend from the point it starts to the point the bend finishes, that radius must be maintained at a minimum to avoid damage to the cable and internal conductors. Choice **a** is incorrect. Choices **c** and **d** are incorrect because while six and seven times the diameter of the cable is acceptable, the question asked for the minimum required to comply with the NEC. (NEC 338.24)

73. The correct answer is **c**. Table 430.52 is used to determine the maximum rating or settings of motor branch-circuit, short-circuit, and ground-fault protective devices and is based on percentages of the full-load current found in Tables 430.247 through 430.250. Choice **a** is incorrect because Section 430.72(B) addresses the sizing of overcurrent protective devices for motor control circuits. The question asks for the table that addresses the maximum rating or settings of motor branch-circuit, short-circuit, and ground-fault protective devices, which is covered in Section 430.52. Choice **b** is incorrect because Section 430.62 addresses the motor short-circuit and ground faults for feeders. The question asks about branch circuits. Choice **d** is incorrect because Section 430.22(E) and its associated table are about various duty cycle percentages that are applied depending on the duty cycle of the motor. (NEC 430, Table 430.52)

74. The correct answer is **b**. According to Table 430.250, the FLC of a 40-HP, three-phase motor at 460 volts is 52 amps. Choices **a**, **c**, and **d** are incorrect. (NEC Table 430.250)

75. The correct answer is **d**. As stated in Section 430.36, the fuse location is to be installed specifically in ungrounded conductors and grounded conductors if the supply system is a 3-wire, 3-phase AC system with one conductor grounded. Choice **a** is incorrect because any bonding conductors used in conjunction with a motor would not have a fuse installed in series with it. The question asks about actual fuse locations to be installed in grounded conductors if the supply system is a 3-wire, 3-phase AC system with one conductor grounded. Choice **b** is incorrect because any grounding conductors used in conjunction with a motor would not have a fuse installed in series with it. The question asks about actual fuse locations to be installed in grounded conductors if the supply system is a 3-wire, 3-phase AC system with one conductor grounded. Choice **c** is incorrect because a fuse holder is always used to hold the fuse itself, so the question asks about the location where a fuse is to be located. The fuse holder is the mid-point of the line and load locations on a circuit, but the fuse itself is protecting the conductors and in this case also serving as the overload for the motor, where applicable. (NEC 430.36)

76. The correct answer is **c**. In order to adequately protect all aspects of a branch circuit, the device which provides overcurrent protection dictates that rating of the circuit. Choice **a** is incorrect because while circuits should be sized in accordance with the anticipated connected load, it is the overcurrent protection device that indicates the rating of the circuit. Choice **b** is incorrect because branch circuit conductors must be sized so as not to exceed their maximum current rating. However, it is the overcurrent protection device that indicates the rating of the circuit. Choice **d** is incorrect because while circuits should be sized in accordance with the antici-pated connected load, including utilization equip-ment, it is the overcurrent protection device that indicates the rating of the circuit. (NEC 210.18)

77. The correct answer is **a**. It is extremely impor-tant to know the electrical equipment or utiliza-tion equipment that the disconnection means controls. The NEC demands that each discon-nection means be legibly marked to indicate its purpose. However, it may be located in a posi-tion that clearly indicates what it controls. Choice **b** is incorrect because the NEC demands that each disconnection means be legibly marked to indicate its purpose. However, it may be located in a position that clearly indicates what it controls. Choice **c** is incorrect because while being labeled can go hand in hand with a marking, it does not lend itself to the legibility aspect of the requirement. Even if the equip-ment the disconnect is serving is evident, it still requires labeling. Being "legibly marked" ensures the end user understands the label or markings clearly. Choice **d** is incorrect because it is extremely important to know the electrical equipment or utilization equipment that the disconnection means controls. The NEC demands that each disconnection means be leg-ibly marked to indicate its purpose. However, it may be located in a position that clearly indi-cates what it controls. (NEC 110.22(A))

78. The correct answer is **a**. Section 110.25 addresses the lockable in the open position disconnection means requirements and has been relocated to Article 110 in the 2014 NEC for clarity. Choice **b** is incorrect because Section 422.31(B) refers the user back to Section 110.25 for the lockable disconnection means requirements. Choice **c** is incorrect because Section 430.102(A) addresses the requirement to provide disconnects to all controllers and their location in sight of the controllers. Choice **d** is incorrect because Section 430.102(A) addresses the within-sight requirements for disconnections means associated with motors and controllers. It does not address the lockable in the open position requirements. (NEC 110.25)

79. The correct answer is **b**. The correct wording for the PV power source is WARNING: PHOTOVOLTAIC POWER SOURCE. Choice **a** is incorrect because generally, PV power-source conductors would not be considered a hazard, but since they are connected to PV systems that are always generating power when exposed to illumination, they could be considered a hazard. However, the wording required is specific in Section 690.31(G)(3), and it is WARNING: PHOTOVOLTAIC POWER SOURCE. Choice **c** is incorrect because while it is true that all of the raceways and boxes expressed in the question have PV power-source conductors enclosed within them, the wording required is specific in Section 690.31(G)(3), and it is WARNING: PHOTOVOLTAIC POWER SOURCE. Choice **d** is incorrect because the wording is WARNING: PHOTOVOLTAIC POWER SOURCE. (NEC 690.31(G)(3))

80. The correct answer is **d**. Since we know that PV systems will produce a current any time they are exposed to a light source, the currents that they can produce are considered to be continuous in terms of calculation of a PV system's conductor ampacity. Choices **a** and **b** are incorrect because it is true that PV output and source circuits are in many cases unprotected or remain energized when fire fighters attempt to attack fires on roofs where PV systems are installed. However, in the 2014 NEC, a new provision for rapid shutdown was introduced that will shut down a PV system under specific conditions. PV systems are installed all over the world and are considered very safe when installed in accordance with the manufacturer's instructions and the National Electrical Code. Choice **c** is incorrect because these PV systems have been used since the early 1970s and are considered very reliable when installed properly. They produce a constant supply of energy that is inverted from DC to AC and either supplied back to the utility or used on stand-alone systems for a wide variety of applications. (NEC 690.8(B))

Questions answered correctly _____

Questions answered incorrectly _____

Passing score = minimum of 70%, or 56+ questions correctly.

PRACTICE TEST 3

This practice exam was designed to reflect the format, level, specifications, and content found on typical state tests for Journeyman Electrician certification/licensing. It contains questions based on the 2017 National Electrical Code and related electrical theory.

Official Journeyman Electrician examinations are typically open book tests. This means that you will be allowed to bring and reference any bound copy of the *National Electrical Code® 2017 Edition* during testing. You should also feel free to do so for this practice examination, but it is highly recommended that you check with your state's licensing board to confirm your state's specific testing requirements and allowances.

The official tests are typically four hours (240 minutes). If you would like to practice answering questions under test-like conditions, be sure to set a timer and take the exam in a quiet place where you will be undisturbed for the duration.

After you are finished, evaluate how you did with the answers and explanations immediately following the practice test. Your scores will be based on the number of questions you have answered correctly. A passing score is a minimum of 70%, so your goal is to answer a minimum of 56 questions correctly.

Good luck!

1. Equipment that is capable of being reached quickly for operation, renewal, or inspections without requiring those to whom ready access is requisite to actions such as to use tools (other than keys), to climb over or under, to remove obstacles, or to resort to portable ladders, and so forth is considered _____.
   a. properly installed
   b. accessible
   c. approved
   d. readily accessible

2. A service disconnecting means shall not be installed in _____.
   a. basements
   b. garages
   c. bathrooms
   d. closets

3. Three-way and four-way switches shall be wired so that all switching is done in only the _____.
   a. ungrounded circuit conductors
   b. grounded circuit conductors
   c. black circuit conductors
   d. grounding circuit conductors

4. Dry-type transformers installed indoors and rated _____ or less shall have a separation of at least 300 mm (12 in.) from combustable material unless separated from the combustible material by a fire-resistant, heat-insulated barrier.
   a. 25 kVA
   b. 50 kVA
   c. $72\frac{1}{2}$ kVA
   d. $112\frac{1}{2}$ kVA

5. The NEC states that where connected to a branch circuit having a rating in excess of _____ amperes, lampholders shall be of the heavy-duty type.
   a. 15
   b. 20
   c. 30
   d. 40

6. A motor's nameplate has a locked rotor code letter K; this indicates that the motor will experience _____ kilovolt-amperes per horsepower under a locked rotor condition.
   a. 3.55–3.99
   b. 5.0–5.59
   c. 8.0–8.99
   d. 12.5–13.99

7. What is the maximum allowable overcurrent protection for a 10 AWG, copper, THHN conductor?
   a. 25 amperes
   b. 30 amperes
   c. 35 amperes
   d. 40 amperes

8. Conductors of different systems, rated 1,000 volts or less, shall be permitted to occupy the same equipment wiring enclosure, cable, or raceway if all conductors have a(n) _____ rating equal to at least the maximum circuit voltage applied to any of the other conductors installed.
   a. insulation
   b. voltage
   c. ampere
   d. overcurrent protection device

9. An individual disconnecting means shall be provided for each controller and shall disconnect the controller. The disconnecting means shall be _____ the controller.
   a. an integral part of
   b. located adjacent to
   c. located on the same premises as
   d. located in sight from

10. The ampacity of feeders supplying a combination of transformers and utilization equipment shall not be less than the sum of the nameplate ratings of the transformers and _____ percent of the designed potential load of the utilization equipment that will be operated simultaneously.
    a. 80
    b. 100
    c. 125
    d. 175

11. With regard to enclosures, the operating handle of a circuit breaker shall be permitted to be _____ without opening a door or cover.
    a. enclosed
    b. energized
    c. exposed
    d. accessible

12. The requirements for connection to ground, for the metal-sheathed or armored underground service cable can be found in part _____ of Article 250 – Grounding and Bonding.
    a. Part II
    b. Part III
    c. Part IV
    d. Part VI

13. The definition of *Alternate Power Source* can be found in Article _____.
    a. 100
    b. 230
    c. 517
    d. 690

14. A 120V, overhead cable, supported on a solidly grounded messenger conductor must not be run within _____ ft. of the water level of a pool.
    a. 10
    b. 22.5
    c. 25
    d. 27

15. Electrical Nonmetallic Tubing (ENT) shall be securely fastened at intervals not exceeding _____.
    a. 12 inches
    b. 24 inches
    c. 36 inches
    d. 48 inches

16. For a voltage drop calculation, what is the resistance of 160 ft. of 12 AWG solid copper conductor?
    a. 0.3088 Ω
    b. 0.3216 Ω
    c. 0.3168 Ω
    d. 1.672 Ω.

17. Overtemperature limit control requirements for electrode-type boilers can be found in NEC section _____.
    a. 422.11
    b. 424.73
    c. 424.83
    d. 424.84

18. Live parts of generators operated at more than _____ volts AC to ground shall not be exposed to accidental contact where accessible to unqualified persons.
a. 25
b. 50
c. 120
d. 240

19. Emergency systems shall be tested periodically on a schedule acceptable to the _____ to ensure the systems are maintained in proper operating condition.
a. local fire marshal
b. building supervisor
c. designing architect
d. authority having jurisdiction

20. According to NEC Section _____, "Electrical equipment shall be installed in a neat and workmanlike manner."
a. 90.7
b. 110.12
c. 210.5
d. 300.21

21. Temporary electric power and lighting installations shall be permitted for a period not to exceed _____ days for holiday decorative lighting and similar purposes.
a. 30
b. 60
c. 90
d. 120

22. The minimum cover requirements for a GFCI protected, 120V, residential branch circuit rated 15 amperes is _____ inches.
a. 24
b. 18
c. 12
d. 6

23. Receptacles rated 20 amperes or less and designed for the direct connection of aluminum conductors shall be marked _____.
a. CO/ALR
b. CU/AL
c. either CO/ALR or CU/AL
d. aluminum conductors shall not be used

24. The section of the NEC that provides the requirements for 125-volt, 15- and 20-ampere receptacle outlets in dwelling units is _____.
a. 210.11(C)
b. 210.19(A)
c. 210.50
d. 210.52

25. For feeders, the _____, if insulated, shall be identified in accordance with Section 200.6 of the NEC.
a. ungrounded conductor
b. insulated conductor
c. grounded conductor
d. grounding conductor

26. The maximum demand for one 11.5 kW household electric range is _____ kW.
a. 8
b. 9.2
c. 11
d. 11.5

27. For an outdoor fuel dispensing facility, the area 18 inches above grade level, and extending 20 feet horizontally in all directions from the dispenser enclosure, is classified as _____.
a. Class I, Division 1
b. Class II, Division 2
c. Division 1, Zone 1
d. Division 2, Zone 2

28. Type NM cable shall be permitted to be _____.
  a. used in outside walls of masonry block or tile
  b. concealed in moist, damp, or corrosive locations
  c. fished in air voids in masonry block or tile walls
  d. embedded in poured concrete

29. When sizing a short-circuit and ground-fault protective device for a single-phase motor, the NEC allows the maximum rating of the _____ to be 800 percent of the motor's full-load current rating.
  a. nontime delay fuse
  b. dual element fuse
  c. instantaneous trip breaker
  d. inverse time breaker

30. Insulated conductors used for connections between resistance elements and controllers shall be suitable for an operating temperature of no less than _____.
  a. 90°C (194°F)
  b. 75°C (167°F)
  c. 60°C (149°F)
  d. Both a and b

31. The allowable ampacity of a 300 kcmil RHW copper conductor, installed in a raceway with two other current-carrying conductors, in an environment where the ambient temperature is 85°F, is _____ amperes.
  a. 320
  b. 285
  c. 240
  d. 230

32. At least 6" of free conductor, measured from _____, shall be left at each outlet, junction, and switch point for splices or connection of luminaires or devices.
  a. the point where the conductors emerge for the box
  b. the point in the box where it emerges from the raceway or cable sheath
  c. the point where the cable or raceway enters the box
  d. the point where the cable or raceway emerges from the connector

33. Cartridge fuses in circuits of any voltage where accessible to other than qualified persons, and all fuses in circuits over 150 volts to ground, shall be provided with a disconnecting means on the _____ side so that each circuit containing fuses can be independently disconnected from the source of power.
  a. supply
  b. load
  c. primary
  d. secondary

34. Determine the current through the circuit below with an applied voltage of 120 volts and total resistance of 20 Ω.

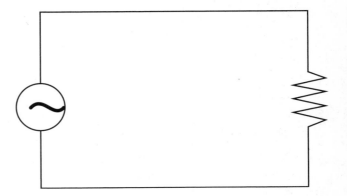

  a. 0.167 amperes
  b. 0.6 amperes
  c. 6 amperes
  d. 2,400 amperes

35. Where installed in a metal raceway or other metal enclosure, all conductors of all feeders using a common neutral conductor shall be enclosed within the same raceway or other enclosure as required in _____.
a. 110.6
b. 215.2
c. 300.20
d. 310.15

36. Conductors of _____ shall not be intermixed in a terminal or splicing connector where physical contact occurs between them.
a. dissimilar voltage ratings
b. dissimilar insulation temperature ratings
c. dissimilar sizes
d. dissimilar metals

37. For electric arc welders, a rating plate shall be provided listing all of the following information except _____.
a. primary wattage
b. frequency
c. rated secondary current
d. name of manufacturer

38. The voltage correction factor for a crystalline photovoltaic module, operating in an ambient temperature of 2°F is _____.
a. 1.06
b. 1.10
c. 1.18
d. 1.23

39. Where mating dissimilar metals at battery and cell terminations, _____ suitable for the battery connection shall be used where recommended by the battery manufacturer.
a. antioxidant material
b. conductors
c. terminals
d. lubricant material

40. The maximum number of 14 AWG conductors that can be installed in a $4 \times 2\frac{1}{8}$ in. metal square box is _____.
a. 9
b. 10
c. 13
d. 15

41. For calculating the lighting load for specified occupancies, the _____ shall be multiplied by square footage of the occupancy calculated by the outside dimensions of each floor.
a. amperage
b. unit load
c. area
d. total load

42. The letter designation of R, on the insulation of a conductor, indicates that the insulation is _____.
a. suitable for wet locations
b. thermoplastic
c. thermoset
d. 75°C

43. A flexible metal conduit shall be securely fastened in place by approved means at intervals not to exceed _____ feet and within 12 inches of each outlet box.
a. 2
b. $3\frac{1}{2}$
c. $4\frac{1}{2}$
d. 6

44. The size of conductors supplying equipment covered by Article 430 shall be selected from the allowable ampacity tables in accordance with _____.
a. 310.15(B)
b. 400.5
c. 430.6(A), (B), (C), and (D)
d. 430.72(B)

45. Service conductors shall have a clearance of no less than _____ inches from windows that are designed to be opened.
  a. 24
  b. 30
  c. 36
  d. 48

46. A receptacle installed outdoors in a location protected from the weather or in other damp locations shall have an enclosure for the receptacle that is _____ when the receptacle is covered.
  a. raintight
  b. rainproof
  c. weathertight
  d. weatherproof

47. A switchbox installed in a plaster wall may be recessed no more than _____ inches from the finished surface of the wall.
  a. $\frac{1}{16}$
  b. $\frac{1}{8}$
  c. $\frac{1}{4}$
  d. 0

48. Below is the symbol that is commonly found on plans and wiring diagrams depicting a _____.

  a. duplex receptacle outlet
  b. single receptacle outlet
  c. lighting outlet
  d. split receptacle outlet

49. Each multiwire branch circuit shall be provided with a means that will _____ all ungrounded conductors at the point where the branch circuit originates.
  a. individually disconnect
  b. simultaneously disconnect
  c. instantaneously disconnect
  d. automatically disconnect

50. A conductor's American Wire Gauge number (AWG) gets smaller as the ampacity of the conductor _____.
  a. stays the same
  b. decreases
  c. increases
  d. none of the above

51. When applying continuous loads, electricians should consult NEC Article _____.
  a. 100
  b. 314
  c. 430
  d. 550

52. How many conductors are needed from a standard 120/240-volt, single-phase, dwelling service panelboard enclosure to a remotely located distribution panel in the same building?
  a. two
  b. three
  c. four
  d. six

53. An electrician would reference section _____ of the NEC in order to determine the uses permitted for surface nonmetallic raceway installations.
  a. 376.10
  b. 378.10
  c. 386.10
  d. 388.10

54. What is the allowable receptacle rating(s) for a multi-receptacle branch circuit with an over-current protective device rated 20 amperes?
 a. 15 amperes
 b. 20 amperes
 c. Either **a** or **b**
 d. Neither **a** nor **b**

55. The uses permitted for lamp cord include all but _____.
 a. hard usage
 b. dry locations
 c. pendants
 d. portable

56. _____ are the conductors between the interactive inverter and the service equipment or another electric power production source, such as a utility, for electrical production and distribution networks.
 a. Inverter output circuits
 b. Inverter input circuits
 c. Interactive output circuits
 d. Interactive input circuits

57. Overcurrent protection for legally required standby systems is found in Part _____ of Article 701.
 a. I
 b. II
 c. III
 d. IV

58. For electrical metallic tubing (EMT), there shall not be more than the equivalent of four quarter bends (_____ degrees total) between pull points.
 a. 360
 b. 270
 c. 180
 d. 90

59. A supplemental grounding electrode is required for all but _____ type of grounding electrodes.
 a. a single rod
 b. a single ground ring
 c. a single pipe
 d. a single plate

60. The identification of terminals to which a grounded conductor is to be connected shall be _____.
 a. marked appropriately
 b. any approved color
 c. substantially white
 d. substantially silver

61. Alternating-current systems of 50–1,000 volts that supply premises wiring and premises wiring systems shall be grounded under all but which of the following conditions?
 a. where the system is used exclusively to supply industrial electric furnaces for melting, refining, tempering, and the like
 b. where the system can be grounded so that the maximum voltage to ground on the ungrounded conductors does not exceed 150 volts
 c. where the system is 3-phase, 4-wire, wye connected in which the neutral conductor is used as a circuit conductor
 d. where the system is 3-phase, 4-wire, delta connected in which the midpoint of one phase winding is used as a circuit conductor

62. For a hermetic refrigerant motor-compressor, the _____ marked on the nameplate of the equipment shall be used in determining the rating or ampacity of the disconnecting means, the branch-circuit conductors, and the branch-circuit short-circuit and ground-fault protection.
 a. rated voltage
 b. locked rotor current
 c. rated load current
 d. horse-power rating

63. In both exposed and concealed locations where nonmetallic-sheathed cables pass through either factory- or field-punched, cut, or drilled slots or holes in _____, the cable shall be protected by listed bushings or listed grommets covering all metal edges that are securely fastened in the opening prior to installation of the cable.
 a. wooden members
 b. metal members
 c. Both **a** and **b**
 d. Neither **a** nor **b**

64. For underground installations, which of the following shall be sealed or plugged at either or both ends?
 a. conduits
 b. unused raceways
 c. spare raceways
 d. All of the above

65. Table _____ lists references for specific equipment and applications not located in Chapters 5, 6, and 7 that amend or supplement the requirements of Article 210—Branch Circuits.
 a. 210.3
 b. 210.21(B)(2)
 c. 210.21(B)(3)
 d. 210.24

66. For pendants installed above Class I locations in commercial garages, flexible cords shall be listed for _____.
 a. portable power cords
 b. junior hard service
 c. hard usage
 d. thermoplastic parallel cords

67. Busways shall be permitted to be installed vertically through dry floors if totally enclosed where passing through and for a minimum distance of _____ ft. above the floor to provide adequate protection for physical damage.
 a. 2
 b. 4
 c. 5
 d. 6

68. A(n) _____ is the ratio of the maximum demand of a system, or part of a system, to the total connected load of a system or the part of the system under consideration.
 a. demand factor
 b. total load
 c. overload
 d. voltage to ground

69. Seven current-carrying, 250 kcmil XHHW copper conductors are installed together in a raceway under dry conditions. The maximum allowable ampacity for each conductor is _____ amps.
 a. 178.5
 b. 203
 c. 255
 d. 290

70. For a one-family dwelling, the services shall have a rating of not less than _____, 3-wire.
a. 100 amperes
b. 120 volts
c. 200 amperes
d. 240 volts

71. How many overload relays would you need to install in a 3-phase AC circuit suppling a motor?
a. 1
b. 2
c. 3
d. 4

72. Nonmetallic auxiliary gutters shall be listed for the _____ of the installation.
a. intended use
b. maximum ambient temperature
c. minimum ambient temperature
d. installed conductor insulation temperature rating

73. For dwelling units lighting load demand, the first 3000 VA is calculated at _____ %.
a. 25
b. 35
c. 100
d. 125

74. Overhead conductors for festoon lighting shall not be smaller than _____ AWG unless the conductors are supported by messenger wires.
a. 18
b. 16
c. 14
d. 12

75. Type AC cable and its associated fittings shall be _____.
a. listed
b. approved
c. accessible
d. All of the above

76. Where rigid polyvinyl chloride (PVC) conduit is installed in a straight run, in an area that can expect to experience up to a 30° F temperature change over time, a thermal expansion of _____ in./100 ft. must be compensated for by the use of an expansion fitting.
a. 0.20
b. 1.22
c. 1.83
d. 5.27

77. Ampacities for conductors shall be determined by tables as provided in 310.15(B) or _____.
a. from the designing architect
b. listed by the manufacture
c. provided by the AHJ
d. under engineering supervision

78. Allowable ampacity for fixture wires shall be specified in Table _____.
a. 310.15(B)(16)
b. 310.15(B)(19)
c. 400.5(A)(1)
d. 402.5

79. Hazardous locations shall be classified by the presence of substances that are deemed dangerous. Which of the following properties are included in this list?
a. flammable gas
b. combustible liquid-produced vapor
c. fibers/flyings
d. All of the above

80. Branch circuits recognized by Article 210 shall be rated in accordance with _____.
　a. the maximum allowable ampacity of the conductors
　b. the rating of the devices and equipment
　c. the maximum permitted ampere rating of the overcurrent device
　d. All of the above

Answers and Explanations

1. The correct answer is **d**. Choice **a** is incorrect because there is no definition for *properly installed* and there are many factors that dictate a proper installation. Choice **b** is incorrect because equipment that is *accessible* is that which is installed to allow close approach. Choice **c** is incorrect because *approved* means acceptable to the authority having jurisdiction. (NEC 100)

2. The correct answer is **c**. Choices **a**, **b**, and **d** are incorrect because service disconnecting means shall not be installed in bathrooms. (NEC 230.70(A)(2))

3. The correct answer is **a**. To ensure that no voltage is present at a device or piece of equipment, switching is done only in the ungrounded circuit conductors. Choice **b** is incorrect because this would create an unsafe condition where voltage would be present at a device or piece of equipment when the load was turned off. Choice **c** is incorrect because switching may be done in conductors of various colors; while black is acceptable it is not the only acceptable color. Choice **d** is incorrect because under no circumstances would it be permitted or desirable for switching to be done in the grounding conductor. This would create an unsafe condition and would not control the load. (NEC 404.2(A))

4. The correct answer is **d**. Choice **a** is incorrect because dry-type transformers installed indoors and rated $112\frac{1}{2}$ kVA or less shall have a separation of at least 300 mm (12 in.) from combustible material unless separated from the combustible material by a fire-resistant, heat-insulated barrier. While 25 kVA meets the requirement, it does not satisfy the condition stated in the question. Choice **b** is incorrect because while 50 kVA meets the requirement, it does not satisfy the condition stated in the question. Choice **c** is incorrect because while $72\frac{1}{2}$ kVA meets the requirement, it does not satisfy the condition stated in the question. (NEC 450.21(A))

5. The correct answer is **b**. Choices **a**, **c**, and **d** are incorrect because, where connected to a branch circuit in excess of 20 amperes, lampholders shall be of the heavy-duty type. (NEC 210.21(A))

6. The correct answer is **c**. Code letter K indicates the motor will experience 8.0–8.99 kilovolt-amperes per horsepower under locked rotor conditions. (NEC Table 430.7(B))

7. The correct answer is **b**. While Table 310.16(B)(16) lists the allowable ampacity of a 10 AWG copper THHN conductor as 40 amperes, the double asterisk adjacent to the conductor size refers us to NEC 240.4(D) for maximum overcurrent protection. The maximum overcurrent protection for this conductor is 30 amperes. Choice A is incorrect because overcurrent protection of 25 amperes is allowable for a 10 AWG copper THHN conductor. However, the maximum rating is 30 amperes. Choice **c** is incorrect because a 35 ampere overcurrent protection device exceeds the maximum allowable rating, which is 30 amperes. Choice **d** is incorrect because a 40 ampere overcurrent protection device exceeds the maximum allowable rating, which is 30 amperes. (NEC 240.4(D)(7))

8. The correct answer is **a**. All conductors that occupy the same equipment wiring enclosure, cable, or raceway must have the same insulation rating as that of the conductor with the highest applied voltage. Choice **b** is incorrect because voltage rating is one of the parameters of a conductor's insulation rating and must be considered when installing conductors of different systems in the same equipment wiring enclosure, cable, or raceway. However, choosing this response does not completely satisfy the question as it does not take into account the other parameters such as temperature, suitable locations (wet, damp, or dry), etc. Choice **c** is incorrect because ampere rating is not one of the parameters of a conductor's insulation rating and need not be considered when installing conductors of different systems in the same equipment wiring enclosure, cable, or raceway. Choice **d** is incorrect because overcurrent protection device rating is not one of the parameters of a conductor's insulation rating and need not be considered when installing conductors of different systems in the same equipment wiring enclosure, cable, or raceway. (NEC 300.3(C)(1))

9. The correct answer is **d**. An individual disconnecting means shall be located in sight from the controller. Choice **a** is incorrect because while it would be allowable to have a disconnecting means as an integral part of a controller, it is not the requirement of the NEC. An individual disconnecting means shall be located in sight from the controller. Choice **b** is incorrect because while it would be allowable to have a disconnecting means located adjacent to a controller, it is not the requirement of the NEC. An individual disconnecting means shall be located in sight from the controller. Choice **c** is incorrect because this response is too vague. The disconnecting means would certainly be located on the same premises as the controller. However, this answer implies that it could be anywhere on the premises. An individual disconnecting means shall be located in sight from the controller. (NEC 430.102(A))

10. The correct answer is **c**. The ampacity of these feeders shall be not less than 100 percent of the nameplate rating of the transformer, added to 125 percent of the designed load of the utilization equipment. Choice **a** is incorrect because allowing for only 80 percent of the designed load of the utilization equipment would grossly undersize the ampacity of the feeder. The ampacity of these feeders shall be not less than 100 percent of the nameplate rating of the transformer, added to 125 percent of the designed load of the utilization equipment. Choice **b** is incorrect because allowing for only 100 percent of the designed load of the utilization equipment does not take into account the possibility of the equipment operating continuously, and thus would undersize the ampacity of the feeder. The ampacity of these feeders shall be not less than 100 percent of the nameplate rating of the transformer, added to 125 percent of the designed load of the utilization equipment. Choice **d** is incorrect because allowing for 175 percent of the designed load of the utilization equipment would oversize the ampacity of the feeder. While this would not be in violation of the NEC, it is not the most efficient practice in terms of the cost of materials and labor. The ampacity of these feeders shall be not less than 100 percent of the nameplate rating of the transformer, added to 125 percent of the designed load of the utilization equipment. (NEC 215.2(B)(2))

11. The correct answer is **d**. According to NEC 240.30(B), the operating handle may be accessible without opening a door or cover. Choice **a** is incorrect because this answer is redundant as the question is asked with regard to enclosures. According to NEC 240.30(B), the operating handle may be accessible without opening a door or cover. Choice **b** is incorrect because the circuit breaker may or may not be energized. Choice **c** is incorrect because the circuit breaker may or may not be exposed.

12. The correct answer is **c**. Part IV addresses Enclosures, Raceways, and Service Cable Connections. Choice **a** is incorrect because Part II addresses grounding for entire electrical systems, and not particular raceways or cables. Choice **b** is incorrect because Part III addresses the Grounding Electrode System and Conductors. Choice **d** is incorrect because Part VI addresses equipment grounding and conductors used for this purpose.

13. The correct answer is **c**. The phrase *Alternate Power Source* can only be found in Article 517— Health Care Facilities of the NEC. Choices **a** and **b** are incorrect. Choice **b** is incorrect because Article 230 addresses Services. Choice **d** is incorrect because Article 690 addresses Photovoltaic (PV) Systems. (NEC 517.2))

14. The correct answer is **b**. Overhead clearance for a 120V cable on a solidly grounded messenger conductor is 22.5 ft. Choice **a** is incorrect because this would be dangerous, as it would allow the overhead cable to get too close to the surface of the water. Choice **c** is incorrect because 25 ft. satisfies the NEC requirement for safety, but it does not answer the question as it is being asked. Choice **d** is incorrect because 27 ft. satisfies the NEC requirement for safety, but it does not answer the question as it is being asked. (NEC Table 680.9(A))

15. The correct answer is **c**. ENT shall be securely fastened at intervals not exceeding 36 inches (3 ft.). Choice **a** is incorrect because although it is well within the minimum requirement of the NEC to fasten ENT every 12 inches, to do so would be a waste of labor and resources. Choice **b** is incorrect because although it is well within the minimum requirement of the NEC to fasten ENT every 24 inches, to do so would be a waste of labor and resources. Choice **d** is incorrect because ENT is not considered securely fastened at intervals of 48 inches as it is a non-metallic wiring method and subject to sagging if not adequately supported. (NEC 362.30(A))

16. The correct answer is **a**. Referring to Chapter 9, Table 8—Conductor Properties, we find that a 12 AWG solid copper, uncoated conductor has a resistance of 1.93 Ω per 1,000 ft. Since we have 160 ft. of the conductor in our circuit, the total resistance is found using the formula (1.93 Ω × 160 ft.) ÷ 1,000 ft. The correct answer is 0.3088 Ω. Choice **b** is incorrect because in order to find the correct resistance for this conductor, we must refer to Chapter 9, Table 8—Conductor Properties. You must use caution in choosing the appropriate column to obtain resistance per 100 ft. In this case, the resistance for a 12 AWG solid copper, *coated* conductor was used. This conductor has a resistance of 2.01 Ω per 1,000 ft. Thus, using the formula (2.01 Ω × 160 ft.) ÷ 1,000 ft. = 0.3216 Ω. The correct column to use is that for uncoated conductor, which provides a resistance of 1.93 Ω per 1,000 ft. Choice **c** is incorrect because in this case, the resistance for a 12 AWG *stranded* copper, uncoated conductor was used. This conductor has a resistance of 1.98 Ω per 1,000 ft. Thus, using the formula (1.98 Ω × 160 ft.) ÷ 1,000 ft. = 0.3168 Ω. Choice **d** is incorrect because this conductor has a resistance of 10.45 Ω per 1,000 ft. Thus, using the formula (10.45 Ω × 160 ft.) ÷ 1,000 ft. = 1.672 Ω. The correct column to use is that for solid, copper, uncoated conductor, which provides a resistance of 1.93 Ω per 1,000 ft. (NEC Ch.9 Table 8).

17. The correct answer is **c**. Each boiler shall be equipped with a temperature-sensitive limiting means, which is installed to protect against liquid temperatures exceeding maximum safe limits. Choice **a** is incorrect because Section 422.11 addresses overcurrent protection for appliances. Choice **b** is incorrect because Section 424.73 addresses overtemperature limit control for resistance-type boilers. Choice **d** is incorrect because Section 424.84 addresses overpressure limit control for electrode-type boilers. (NEC 424.83)

18. The correct answer is **b**. A generator operated at more than 50 volts AC to ground shall have protection of live parts. Choice **a** is incorrect because a generator operated at 25 volts AC to ground does not require protection of live parts. Choice **c** is incorrect because a generator operated at more than 120 volts AC to ground shall have protection for live parts. However, this is not the minimum voltage addressed in this section. Choice **d** is incorrect because a generator operated at more than 240 volts AC to ground shall have protection for live parts. However, this is not the minimum voltage addressed in this section. (NEC 445.14)

19. The correct answer is **d**. The authority having jurisdiction is the person responsible for approving the testing schedule for Emergency Systems. Choice **a** is incorrect because although the local fire marshal may be the authority having jurisdiction in some locations, this may not be true for all. Choice **b** is incorrect because although the building supervisor may be the authority having jurisdiction in some locations, this may not be true for all. Choice **c** is incorrect because the designing architect is never the authority having jurisdiction. (NEC 700.3(B))

20. The correct answer is **b**. Section 110.12 is entitled the Mechanical Execution of Work, and states "Electrical equipment shall be installed in a neat and workmanlike manner." Choice **a** is incorrect because Section 90.7 addresses examination of equipment for safety. Choice **c** is incorrect because Section 210.5 addresses identification for branch circuit conductors. Choice **d** is incorrect because Section 300.21 addresses the spread of fire or products of combustion. (NEC 100.12)

21. The correct answer is **c**. Temporary electrical power and lighting installations shall be permitted to be installed for a maximum of 90 days. Choice A is incorrect because while temporary electrical power and lighting installations would be permitted to be installed for 30 days, this is not the maximum length of time that is permissible, which is 90 days. Choice **b** is incorrect because while temporary electrical power and lighting installations would be permitted to be installed for 60 days, this is not the maximum length of time that is permissible, which is 90 days. Choice **d** is incorrect because temporary electrical power and lighting installations shall be permitted to be installed for a maximum of 90 days; 120 days would be in violation to the code. (NEC 590.3(B))

22. The correct answer is **c**. The minimum required depth to install a residential branch circuit, rated 15 amperes, 120 volts, and GFCI protected is 12 inches. Choice **a** is incorrect because it would be permissible to install a residential branch circuit, rated 15 amperes, 120 volts, and GFCI protected at 24 inches. However, the minimum required depth is 12 inches. Choice **b** is incorrect because it would be permissible to install a residential branch circuit, rated 15 amperes, 120 volts, and GFCI protected at 18 inches. However, the minimum required depth is 12 inches. Choice **d** is incorrect because it would not be permissible to install a residential branch circuit, rated 15 amperes, 120 volts, and GFCI protected at 6 inches, as the minimum required depth is 12 inches. (NEC Table 300.5)

23. The correct answer is **a**. Receptacles rated 20 amperes or less and designed for the direct connection of aluminum conductors shall be marked CO/ALR. Choice **b** is incorrect because CU and AL are the symbols found on the Periodic Table of Elements for copper and aluminum respectively. This designation was originally used on devices to indicate suitability for aluminum conductors. However, testing discovered that this was not the case for devices rated 20 amperes or less. New devices with larger screw terminals were developed and marked with the designation of CO/ALR, which is now code compliant. Choice **c** is incorrect because CO/ALR is the only acceptable designation for receptacles rated 20 amperes or less that are intended for the direct connection to aluminum conductors. Choice **d** is incorrect because aluminum conductors may be directly connected to receptacles rated 20 amperes or less that have a designation of CO/ALR. (NEC 406.3(C))

24. The correct answer is **d**. Section 210.52 contains all of the requirements for 125-volt, 15- and 20-ampere receptacle outlets in dwelling units. Choice **a** is incorrect because Section 210.11(C) contains the branch circuit requirements for dwelling units. Choice **b** is incorrect because Section 210.19(A) contains the minimum ampacity and size of conductors installed on branch circuits rated not more than 600 volts. Choice **c** is incorrect because Section 210.50 contains the general requirements for other occupancies and uses, not just dwelling units. (NEC 210.52)

25. The correct answer is **c**. The grounded conductor, which may also be considered the "neutral" conductor for a feeder circuit, shall be identified in accordance with Section 200.6. Choice **a** is incorrect because Section 200.6 provides the means of identifying grounded conductors. Choice **b** is incorrect because all of the conductors of a feeder circuit shall be insulated except for the grounding conductor. Section 200.6 provides the means of identifying grounded conductors. Choice **d** is incorrect because Section 200.6 provides the means of indentifying grounded conductors. (215.12(A))

26. The correct answer is **a**. According to Column **c** of Table 220.55, for household electric ranges not over 12 kW, the maximum demand is 8 kW. Choice **b** is incorrect because for other than continuous duty loads, applying the 80% rule is often appropriate. 80% of 11.5 kW equals 9.2kW. While it would not be hazardous to use this demand for the range in question, it would result in oversizing the circuit's overcurrent protection and conductors, and would be a waste of resources. Choice **c** is incorrect because, referring to Column **c** or Table 220.55, we find the demand for 2 household electric ranges not over 12 kW to be 11 kW. While it would not be hazardous to use this demand for the range in question, it would result in oversizing the circuit's overcurrent protection and conductors, and would be a waste of resources. Choice **d** is incorrect because in this case, no demand is applied. While it would not be hazardous to use this kW rating for the range in question, it would result in oversizing the circuit's overcurrent protection and conductors, and would be a waste of resources. (NEC Table 220.55)

27. The correct answer is **d**. Within the Class I classification, Division 2, Zone 2 is applied to the area 18 inches above grade level, and extending 20 feet horizontally in all directions from the dispenser enclosure. Choice **a** is incorrect because Class I is the correct classification, but Division 1 applies to the area under the dispenser containment area. Choice **b** is incorrect because liquid fuel is considered a Class I substance. Therefore, an area where fuel is dispensed must also be classified as Class I. Choice **c** is incorrect because within the Class I classification, Division 1, Zone 1 is only applied to the area under the dispenser containment area. (NEC Table 514.3(B)(1))

28. The correct answer is **c**. Type NM cable shall be permitted to be installed in fished air voids of masonry block as this would not require protection from physical damage, moisture, or corrosion. Choice **a** is incorrect because Type NM cable offers no physical protection to the conductors which would be required for this application. Choice **b** is incorrect because Type NM cable offers no protection from moisture or corrosion. Choice **d** is incorrect because Type NM cable offers no protection from physical damage or moisture. (NEC 334.10(A)(2))

29. The correct answer is **c**. The maximum rating for an instantaneous trip breaker for a single-phase motor is 800 percent of the motor's full-load current rating. Choice **a** is incorrect because the maximum rating for a non-time delay fuse for a single-phase motor is 300 percent of the motor's full-load current rating. Choice **b** is incorrect because the maximum rating for a dual element fuse for a single-phase motor is 175 percent of the motor's full-load current rating. Choice **d** is incorrect because the maximum rating for an inverse time breaker for a single-phase motor is 250 percent of the motor's full-load current rating. (NEC Table 430.52)

30. The correct answer is **a**. For connections between resistive elements and their controllers, conductors must be of the highest temperature rating. Choices **b** and **c** are incorrect because conductors that provide the connections between resistive elements and their controllers are subjected to very high temperatures due to the resistive load. Therefore, conductors must be of the highest temperature rating. Choice **d** is incorrect because only the **a** portion of this answer is true, making the answer incorrect. (NEC 470.4)

31. The correct answer is **b**. A 300 kcmil RHW copper conductor has an allowable ampacity of 285 amperes. Choice **a** is incorrect because the temperature rating of RHW insulation is 75°C (167°F). For a 300 kcmil copper conductor, an ampacity of 320 amperes is found in the 90°C (194°F) column. Choice **c** is incorrect because an ampacity of 240 amperes is found in the 60°C (140°F) column. Choice **d** is incorrect because a 300 kcmil RHW aluminum conductor has an allowable ampacity of 230 amperes. (NEC Table 310.15(B)(16))

32. The correct answer is **b**. The required 6" of free conductor is measured from the point in the box where it emerges from the raceway. Choice **a** is incorrect because depending on the depth of the box, measuring from the edge of the box could result in very long conductors that could cause overcrowding in the box, resulting in damage to the conductors. Choices **c** and **d** are incorrect because especially in the case of cable installation, using a measurement that includes the cable sheath makes it more difficult to manipulate the conductors inside the box. The cable sheath also takes up additional space inside the box so it is required that its length be limited. (NEC 300.14)

33. The correct answer is **a**. Providing a disconnecting means on the supply side of the fuses allows for them to be safely removed from the circuit while not under load, which could cause a dangerous arc. Choice **b** is incorrect. Choice **c** is incorrect because the term primary is associated with the supply side of a transformer, not a disconnecting means. Choice **d** is incorrect because the term primary is associated with the load side of a transformer, not a disconnecting means. (NEC 240.40)

34. The correct answer is **c**. The correct Ohm's Law formula must be applied to solve for the correct answer, $I = E \div R$ or $6A = 120V \div 20\Omega$. Choice **a** is incorrect because an answer of 0.167 amperes would result in applying the formula incorrectly, that of $I = R \div E$ or $20\Omega \div 120V = 0.167A$. Choice **b** is incorrect because an answer of 0.6 amperes would result from an arithmetic error of not carrying the decimal point far enough to the right. Choice **d** is incorrect because an answer of 2,400 amperes would result in applying the formula incorrectly, that of $I = R \times E$ or $20\Omega \times 120V = 2,400A$. (Ohm's Law)

35. The correct answer is **c**. Section 300.20 requires that all phase conductors and grounded conductors (neutral) of the same circuit or feeder shall be arranged so as to avoid induced currents on metal enclosures and raceways. This is accomplished by grouping them together in the same raceway or enclosure. Choice **a** is incorrect because Section 110.6 mandates how conductor sizes shall be expressed, in American Wire Gage (AWG) or circular mils. This section is relevant for all conductors, not just those of feeders using a common neutral. Choice **b** is incorrect because Section 215.2 is concerned with the minimum rating and size of feeders. This section is relevant for all feeders, not just those using a common neutral. Choice **d** is incorrect because Section 310.15 deals with the ampacity rating of all conductors, including feeders. (NEC 215.4(B))

36. The correct answer is **d**. Conductors of dissimilar metals (such as copper and aluminum) shall not be intermixed in a terminal or splicing connector unless the device is identified for such purposes. Choice **a** is incorrect because conductors of dissimilar voltage ratings may be in contact with each other provided they both meet the minimum voltage rating of the applied circuit. Choice **b** is incorrect because conductors of dissimilar insulation temperature ratings may be in contact with each other provided they both meet the temperature requirements of the applied circuit. Choice **c** is incorrect because conductors of dissimilar sizes may be in contact with each other provided they both meet the minimum ampacity rating of the applied circuit. (NEC 110.14)

37. The correct answer is **a**. There is no wattage rating requirement for the rating plate provided for arc welders. Choice **b** is incorrect because the arc welder frequency is required for the rating plate on the equipment. Choice **c** is incorrect because the arc welder rated secondary current is required for the rating plate on the equipment. Choice **d** is incorrect because the arc welder's manufacturer is required for the rating plate on the equipment. (NEC 630.14)

38. The correct answer is **c**. A voltage correction factor of 1.18 would apply in an ambient temperature of 4 to −4°F. Choice **a** is incorrect because a voltage correction factor of 1.06 would apply in an ambient temperature of 58 to 50°F. Choice **b** is incorrect because a voltage correction factor of 1.10 would apply in an ambient temperature of 2°C. Choice **d** is incorrect because a voltage correction factor of 1.23 would apply in an ambient temperature of −23 to −31°F. (NEC Table 690.7(A))

39. The correct answer is **a**. Where dissimilar metals come in contact with each other, oxidation can occur. Thus, these connections must be protected from corrosion to maintain continuity. Choice **b** is incorrect because conductors do not connect directly to battery terminals; a termination device must be used. Choice **c** is incorrect because while appropriate terminals must be used, in order to prevent corrosion an antioxidant material must be used at the terminations. Choice **d** is incorrect because there are no moving parts at battery terminals, and thus there is no need for lubrication. (NEC 480.4(A))

40. The correct answer is **d**. In order to provide adequate space for each conductor, 15 is the maximum number of 14 AWG conductors that can be installed in a $4 \times 2\frac{1}{8}$ square metal box. Choice **a** is incorrect because although installing 9, 14 AWG conductors in a $4 \times 2\frac{1}{8}$ square metal box is in compliance with the NEC, this is not the maximum number allowed. Choice **b** is incorrect because although installing 10, 14 AWG conductors in a $4 \times 2\frac{1}{8}$ square metal box is in compliance with the NEC, this is not the maximum number allowed. Choice **c** is incorrect because although installing 13, 14 AWG conductors in a $4 \times 2\frac{1}{8}$ square metal box is in compliance with the NEC, this is not the maximum number allowed. (NEC Table 314.16(A))

41. The correct answer is **b**. The unit load, obtained from Table 220.12, is multiplied by the total square footage of an occupancy in order to determine the lighting load. Choice **a** is incorrect because in calculating the total load it is the amperage we are trying to determine, so this answer is incorrect. Choice **c** is incorrect because the area is the square footage of the occupancy. Choice **d** is incorrect because it is the total lighting load that we are trying to determine, by multiplying the unit load by the square footage of the occupancy. (NEC 220.12)

42. The correct answer is **c**. The letter designation of R indicates that the insulation is thermoset. Choice A is incorrect because the letter designation of W indicates that the insulation is suitable for wet locations. Choice **b** is incorrect because the letter designation of T indicates that the insulation is thermoplastic. Choice **d** is incorrect because the letter designation of H usually indicates that the insulation is rated 75°C. (NEC Table 310.104(A))

43. The correct answer is **c**. Supporting flexible metal conduits at intervals not to exceed $4\frac{1}{2}$ feet are adequate. Choice **a** is incorrect because, as the name implies, this type of conduit is flexible and requires adequate support. However, supporting it every 2 feet would be excessive. Choice **b** is incorrect because supporting it every $3\frac{1}{2}$ feet would be excessive. Choice **d** is incorrect because supporting it every 6 feet would not be considered adequate. (NEC 348.30(A))

44. The correct answer is **a**. Conductors supplying equipment covered in Article 430 shall be selected from the allowable ampacity tables in accordance with 310.15(B). Choice **b** is incorrect because where flexible cords are used to supply equipment in Article 430, conductors shall be selected in accordance with 400.5. Choice **c** is incorrect because Sections 430.6(A), (B), (C), and (D) are used to determine the required ampacity and motor ratings for sizing conductors. Choice **d** is incorrect because Section 430.72(B) addresses overcurrent protection of conductors and not the actual sizing. (NEC 430.6)

45. The correct answer is **c**. Placing service conductors 36 inches from an open window is considered to be outside the reach of people. Choice **a** is incorrect because placing service conductors within 24 inches of an open window would be a hazard, as a person could easily reach them. Choice **b** is incorrect because placing service conductors within 30 inches of an open window would be a hazard, as a person could easily reach them. Choice **d** is incorrect because while placing service conductors 48 inches of an open window would be considered safe, it is not the minimum distance. (NEC 230.9(A))

46. The correct answer is **d**. Weatherproof indicates constructed or protected so that exposure to the weather will not interfere with successful operation. Choice **a** is incorrect because raintight indicates protection from beating rain; the installation described is in a protected but damp location. Choice **b** is incorrect because rainproof indicates constructed as to prevent rain from entering. The installation described is in a protected but damp location. Choice **c** is incorrect because weathertight indicates constructed so that moisture will not enter the enclosure. (NEC 406.9(A))

47. The correct answer is **c**. A plaster wall is considered to be flame resistant; therefore, it is acceptable to allow switchboxes to be recessed no more than $\frac{1}{4}$ inches from the finished surface. Choice **a** is incorrect because $\frac{1}{16}$ inches is compliant with the NEC. However, it is not the maximum distance that a switchbox may be recessed in a plaster wall. Choice **b** is incorrect because $\frac{1}{8}$ inches is compliant with the NEC. However, it is not the maximum distance that a switchbox may be recessed in a plaster wall. Choice **d** is incorrect because zero inches, or flush, are ideal and compliant with the NEC. However, it is not the maximum distance that a switchbox may be recessed in a plaster wall. (NEC 314.20)

48. The correct answer is **a**. The American National Standards Institute has designated this symbol to represent a duplex receptacle outlet. Choice **b** is incorrect because the symbol for a single receptacle outlet would only have one vertical line bisecting the circle. Choice **c** is incorrect because the symbol for a lighting outlet would be a circle with four short lines radiating out from the edges of the circle on 4 different sides. Choice **d** is incorrect because the symbol for a split receptacle would show one half of the circle colored in black. (ANSI)

49. The correct answer is **b**. By simultaneously disconnecting all of the ungrounded conductors, a safe scenario is created for an individual to work on the circuit. Choice **a** is incorrect because by individually disconnecting the ungrounded conductors, a dangerous scenario is created where an individual could unexpectedly come in contact with an energized circuit. Choice **c** is incorrect because an instantaneous disconnecting means may be desirable in an overcurrent condition. That is not addressed in this situation. Choice **d** is incorrect because automatically disconnecting all ungrounded conductors would not be desirable and could create a dangerous situation if the circuits are critical for life safety. (NEC 210.4(B))

50. The correct answer is **c**. As the AWG of a conductor decreases, the conductor's ampacity increases. Choice **a** is incorrect because the AWG number of a conductor varies inversely to the ampacity. This means that when ampacity goes up, AWG goes down. Choice **b** is incorrect because the AWG number of a conductor varies inversely to the ampacity. This means that when ampacity goes up, AWG goes down. Choice **d** is incorrect because the AWG number of a conductor varies inversely to the ampacity. This means that when ampacity goes up, AWG goes down. (NEC Table 310.15(B)(16))

51. The correct answer is **a**. Article 100 defines a continuous load as a load where the maximum current is expected to continue for 3 hours or longer. Choice **b** is incorrect because Article 314 addresses outlet, device, pull, and junction boxes and provides little guidance on the topic of *continuous load*. Choice **c** is incorrect because Article 430 addresses motors and does give some guidance on applying values for continuous and non-continuous loads. In order to apply the various conditions, you would need to know the actual definition of a continuous load. Choice **d** is incorrect because Article 550 addresses mobile and manufactured homes and provides little guidance on the topic of *continuous load*. (NEC 100)

52. The correct answer is **c**. Section 250.24(A)(5) prohibits the grounded (neutral) and equipment grounding conductor from being connected together on the load side of the service disconnection means. In the 120/240-volt, single-phase dwelling system, you have two ungrounded (hot) conductors, one grounded (neutral) conductor, and one equipment grounding conductor. Since the question specifies a 120/240-volt, single-phase system, it is clear that four conductors are required to comply with Section 250.24(A)(5). Choices **a**, **b**, and **d** are incorrect. (NEC 250.24(A)(5))

53. The correct answer is **d**. Section 388.10 provides the uses permitted for surface nonmetallic raceways. Choice **a** is incorrect because Section 376.10 provides the uses permitted for metal wireways. Choice **b** is incorrect because Section 378.10 provides the uses permitted for nonmetallic wireways. Choice **c** is incorrect because Section 386.10 provides the uses permitted for surface metal raceways. (NEC 388.10)

54. The correct answer is **c**. Either a 15 or 20 ampere rated receptacle are acceptable because either will prohibit an overload situation that would result from higher rated equipment from being fed by the circuit. Choice **a** is incorrect because a receptacle rated 15 amperes is allowable but it is not the only possible correct answer listed. Choice **b** is incorrect because a receptacle rated 20 amperes is allowable but it is not the only possible correct answer listed. Choice **d** is incorrect because either a 15 or 20 ampere rated receptacle are acceptable—either will prohibit an overload situation that would result from higher rated equipment being fed by the circuit. (NEC Table 210.21(B)(3))

55. The correct answer is **a**. Lamp cord is intended for light duty usage, to supply power to utilization equipment such as lamps and other household items. Choice **b** is incorrect because dry locations are one of the uses permitted for lamp cord. Choice **c** is incorrect because usage as pendants is one that is permitted for lamp cord. Choice **d** is incorrect because portable use is permitted for lamp cord. (NEC Table 400.4)

56. The correct answer is **c**. Choice **a** is incorrect because the inverter output circuit is the conductor connected to the AC output of an inverter. Choice **b** is incorrect because the inverter input circuit is the conductor connected to the DC input of an inverter. Choice **d** is incorrect because there are no conductors referred to as the interactive inverter input circuit. (NEC 690.2)

57. The correct answer is **d**. Part IV of Article 701 contains information about overcurrent protection for legally required standby systems. Choice **a** is incorrect because Part I of Article 701 contains general information about legally required standby systems. Choice **b** is incorrect because Part II of Article 701 contains circuit wiring information for legally required standby systems. Choice **c** is incorrect because Part III of Article 701 contains information for sources of power for legally required standby systems. (NEC 701 Part IV)

58. The correct answer is **a**. For electrical metallic tubing, a quarter bend is equal to 90 degrees. Therefore, four quarter bends equal 360 degrees. Choice **b** is incorrect because 270 degrees is equal to three quarter bends. Choice **c** is incorrect because 180 degrees is equal to two quarter bends. Choice **d** is incorrect because 90 degrees is equal to one quarter bend. (NEC 358.26)

59. The correct answer is **b**. A supplement grounding electrode is not required for a single grounding ring. Choice **a** is incorrect because a supplement grounding electrode is required for a single grounding rod. Choice **c** is incorrect because a supplement grounding electrode is required for a single grounding pipe. Choice **d** is incorrect because a supplement grounding electrode is required for a single grounding plate. (NEC 250.53(A)(2))

60. The correct answer is **c**. The identification of terminals to which a grounded conductor is to be connected shall be substantially white in color. Choice **a** is incorrect because according to the NEC Style Manual, the use of the term *appropriately* would be unenforceable and vague. You would therefore not find this terminology used in the NEC. Choice **b** is incorrect because there is only one approved color, substantially white. Choice **d** is incorrect because although terminals on some devices may appear silver, the NEC states that the identification of terminals to which a grounded conductor is to be connected shall be substantially white in color. (NEC 200.9)

61. The correct answer is **a**. Section 250.21(A)(1) states that this system is not required to be grounded. Choice **b** is incorrect because this system is required to be grounded as stated in Section 250.20(B)(1). Choice **c** is incorrect because this system is required to be grounded as stated in Section 250.20(B)(2). Choice **d** is incorrect because this system is required to be grounded as stated in Section 250.20(B)(3). (NEC 250.20(B))

62. The correct answer is **c**. The rated load current found on the nameplate of a hermetic refrigerant motor-compressor shall be used to determine circuit components. Choice **a** is incorrect because rated voltage is not used to determine circuit components such as rating or ampacity of the disconnecting means, the branch-circuit conductors, and the branch-circuit short-circuit and ground-fault protection. Choice **b** is incorrect because locked rotor current is not used to determine circuit components such as rating or ampacity of the disconnecting means, the branch-circuit conductors, and the branch-circuit short-circuit and ground-fault protection. Choice **d** is incorrect because horse-power rating is not used to determine circuit components such as rating or ampacity of the disconnecting means, the branch-circuit conductors, and the branch-circuit short-circuit and ground-fault protection. (NEC 440.6(A))

63. The correct answer is **b**. Metal framing members present a physical damage threat to the plastic sheath of the cable. Therefore, the cable sheath must be protected by listed bushings or grommets. Choice **a** is incorrect because wooden framing members do not present a physical damage danger for nonmetallic-sheathed cable. Therefore, there is no need for additional protection. Choice **c** is incorrect because only metal framing members present a physical damage threat to the plastic sheath of the cable. Choice **d** is incorrect because metal framing members present a physical damage threat to the plastic sheath of the cable. Therefore, the cable sheath must be protected by listed bushings or grommets. (NEC 300.4(B)(1))

64. The correct answer is **d**. For underground installations, conduits, and unused and spare raceways shall be sealed or plugged at either or both ends. Choice **a** is incorrect because although conduits must be sealed at either or both ends for underground installations, the correct answer is all of the items listed. Choice **b** is incorrect because although unused raceways must be sealed at either or both ends for underground installations, the correct answer is all of the items listed. Choice **c** is incorrect because although spare raceways must be sealed at either or both ends for underground installations, the correct answer is all of the items listed. (NEC 300.5(G))

65. The correct answer is **a**. Table 210.3 lists references for specific equipment and applications not located in Chapters 5, 6, and 7 that amend or supplement the requirements of Article 210—Branch Circuits. Choice **b** is incorrect because Table 210.21(B)(2) lists the maximum cord-and-plug-connected load to receptacle. Choice **c** is incorrect because table 210.21(B)(3) lists receptacle ratings for various size circuits. Choice **d** is incorrect because Table 210.21(B) (2) is a summary of branch circuit requirements. (NEC Table 210.3)

66. The correct answer is **c**. Because these cords are subject to extreme conditions, they must be of the type listed for hard usage. Choices **a**, **c**, and **d** are incorrect; because these cords are subject to extreme conditions, they must be of the type listed for hard usage. (NEC 511.7(A)(2))

67. The correct answer is **d**. 6 ft. provides adequate physical protection for the busways. Choice **a** is incorrect because 2 ft. does not provide enough physical protection for the busways. Choice **b** is incorrect because 4 ft. does not provide enough physical protection for the busways. Choice **c** is incorrect because 5 ft. does not provide enough physical protection for the busways. (NEC 368.10(C)(2))

68. The correct answer is **a**. Demand factors are applied when diversity of an electrical system may create a discrepancy between the actual load versus the total connected load. Choice **b** is incorrect because the total connected load does not take into account any diversity of the load. Choice **c** is incorrect because an overload occurs as a result of too much current flowing in a circuit. Choice **d** is incorrect because voltage to ground is a measure of potential difference between a conductor or voltage source and ground. (NEC 100)

69. The correct answer is **b**. The number of current-carrying conductors in this installation exceeds the allowable ampacities provided in Table 310.15(B)(16). Therefore, you must take the ampacity listed in this table in the 90°C column (for dry installations), and apply an adjustment factor of 70%, provided in Table 310.15(B)(3)(a). The resulting formula is $-290A \times .7 = 203A$. Choice **a** is incorrect because this answer is obtained if the incorrect value is chosen from Table 310.15(B)(16), that from the 75°C column, while applying the correct adjustment factor of 70%. This is the resulting formula and answer: $-255A \times .7 = 178.5A$. Choice **c** is incorrect because this answer is obtained if the incorrect value is chosen from Table 310.15(B)(16), that from the 75°C column, and there is no application of the adjustment factor of 70%. Choice **d** is incorrect as well—this answer is obtained if the correct value is chosen from Table 310.15(B)(16), that from the 90°C column, but there is no application of the adjustment factor of 70%. (NEC Table 310.15(B)(3)(a))

70. The correct answer is **a**. For a one-family dwelling, the service disconnecting means shall have a rating of no less than 100 amperes, 3-wire. Choice **b** is incorrect because 120V is the standard voltage to ground for one-family dwellings. However, services and their disconnecting means are rated in amperes and not voltage. Choice **c** is incorrect because for smaller one-family dwellings, or those that utilize natural gas, such a large service would not be necessary. Choice **d** is incorrect because 240V is the standard voltage phase to phase for one-family dwellings. However, services and their disconnecting means are rated in amperes and not voltage. (NEC 230.79(C))

71. The correct answer is **c**. Since this is a 3-phase system, there are three ungrounded conductors. Each conductor would require its own overload relay. Choice **a** is incorrect because providing overload protection in only 1 ungrounded conductor would not be adequate. Choice **b** is incorrect because providing overload protection in only two ungrounded conductors would not be adequate. Choice **d** is also incorrect. (NEC Table 430.37)

72. The correct answer is **b**. Nonmetallic auxiliary gutters can be made of many nonmetallic substances such as plastic. Plastic will deform if exposed to excessive temperatures. Therefore, nonmetallic auxiliary gutters must be listed for the maximum temperature it will be exposed to. Choice **a** is incorrect because all electrical equipment must be installed and used for the purposes intended. However, this answer is not specific enough about the listing of nonmetallic auxiliary gutters. Choice **c** is incorrect because nonmetallic auxiliary gutters can be made of many nonmetallic substances such as plastic. Plastic will deform if exposed to excessive temperatures. Therefore, nonmetallic auxiliary gutters must be listed for the maximum temperature it will be exposed to. Choice **d** is incorrect because nonmetallic auxiliary gutters must be marked, not listed, for the installed conductor insulation temperature rating. (NEC 366.10(B))

73. The correct answer is **c**. For dwelling units lighting loads, the first 3,000 VA is calculated at 100%. Choice **a** is incorrect because for dwelling units lighting loads, any load in excess of 120,000 VA is calculated at 25%. Choice **b** is incorrect because for dwelling units lighting loads, the load in between 3,001 and 120,000 VA is calculated at 35%. Choice **d** is incorrect because the purpose of demand factors is to allow the use of a value less than the full calculated load. Therefore, applying a demand would not require the increase of the calculated load by 125%. (NEC Table 220.42)

74. The correct answer is **d**. Overhead conductors for festoon lighting shall not be smaller than 12 AWG unless the conductors are supported by messenger wires. Choice **a** is incorrect because an 18 AWG conductor is no more than 0.046 inches in diameter, which is not large enough to provide its own support when used for overhead festoon lighting. Choice **b** is incorrect because a 16 AWG conductor is no more than 0.058 inches in diameter, which is not large enough to provide its own support when used for overhead festoon lighting. Choice **c** is incorrect because a 14 AWG conductor is no more than 0.073 inches in diameter, which is not large enough to provide its own support when used for overhead festoon lighting. (NEC 225.6(B))

75. The correct answer is **a**. Type AC cable and its associated fittings shall be listed. Choice **b** is incorrect because *approved* means acceptable to the authority having jurisdiction. Wiring materials are not approved, but are listed after being tested for a nationally recognized testing laboratory. Choice **c** is incorrect because *accessible* means installed so as to admit close approach. Type AC cable and its associated fittings may be installed in both accessible and inaccessible locations. Choice **d** is incorrect because type AC cable and its associated fittings shall be listed. (NEC 320.6)

76. The correct answer is **b**. An expansion of 1.22 in./ft. is the characteristic associated with an expected temperature change of 30°F. Choice **a** is incorrect because an expansion of 0.20 in./ft. is the characteristic associated with an expected temperature change of 5°F. Choice **c** is incorrect because an expansion of 1.22 in./ft. is the characteristic associated with an expected temperature change of 30°C. Choice **d** is incorrect because an expansion of 5.27 in./ft. is the characteristic associated with an expected temperature change of 130°C. (NEC Table 352.44)

77. The correct answer is **d**. Ampacities for conductors may be determined under engineering supervision as provided in 310.15(C). Choice **a** is incorrect because designing architects do not determine conductor ampacity. Choice **b** is incorrect because the manufacturer does not determine conductor ampacity. Choice **c** is incorrect because the AHJ does not determine conductor ampacity. (NEC 310.15(A)(1))

78. The correct answer is **d**. Table 402.5 specifies the allowable ampacities of fixture wires. Choice **a** is incorrect because Table 310.15(B)(16) specifies the allowable ampacities of not more than three insulated, current-carrying conductors in a raceway, cable, or earth, based on an ambient temperature of 86°F. Choice **b** is incorrect because Table 310.15(B)(19) specifies the allowable ampacities of single insulated conductors in free air, based on an ambient temperature of 104°F. Choice **c** is incorrect because Table 400.5(A)(1) specifies the allowable ampacities for flexible cords and cables, based on an ambient temperature of 86°F.

79. The correct answer is **d**. Flammable gas, combustible liquid-produced vapor, and fibers/flyings are all listed as properties that could constitute the hazardous location classification. Choice **a** is incorrect because flammable gas is one of the properties listed that could constitute the hazardous location classification. However, it is not the only correct response. Choice **b** is incorrect because combustible liquid-produced vapor is one of the properties listed that could constitute the hazardous location classification. However, it is not the only correct response. Choice **c** is incorrect because fibers/flyings is one of the properties listed that could constitute the hazardous location classification. However, it is not the only correct response. (NEC 500.5(A))

80. The correct answer is **c**. Branch circuits recognized by Article 210 shall be rated in accordance with the maximum permitted ampere rating of the overcurrent device. Choice **a** is incorrect because conductor ampacity is not the determining factor in branch circuit ratings because voltage drop and other factors may necessitate the need for larger conductor sizes than would normally be called for. Choice **b** is incorrect because the ratings of the devices and equipment are not the determining factors in branch circuit ratings. It is perfectly acceptable to install a 15 ampere receptacle on a 20 ampere branch circuit. Choice **d** is incorrect because branch circuits recognized by Article 210 shall be rated in accordance with the maximum permitted ampere rating of the overcurrent device. (NEC 210.3)

Questions answered correctly _____

Questions answered incorrectly _____

Passing score = minimum of 70%, or 56+ questions correctly.

5 ▶ PRACTICE TEST 4

This practice exam was designed to reflect the format, level, specifications, and content found on typical state tests for Journeyman Electrician certification/licensing. It contains questions based on the 2017 National Electrical Code and related electrical theory.

Official Journeyman Electrician examinations are typically open book tests. This means that you will be allowed to bring and reference any bound copy of the *National Electrical Code® 2017 Edition* during testing. You should also feel free to do so for this practice examination, but it is highly recommended that you check with your state's licensing board to confirm your state's specific testing requirements and allowances.

The official tests are typically four hours (240 minutes). If you would like to practice answering questions under test-like conditions, be sure to set a timer and take the exam in a quiet place where you will be undisturbed for the duration.

After you are finished, evaluate how you did with the answers and explanations immediately following the practice test. Your scores will be based on the number of questions you have answered correctly. A passing score is a minimum of 70%, so your goal is to answer a minimum of 56 questions correctly.

Good luck!

1. _____ rules of the NEC are those that identify actions that are required or prohibited, and are characterized by the use of the terms *shall* and *shall not*.
   a. Enforceable
   b. Permissive
   c. Mandatory
   d. Explanatory

2. A system or circuit conductor that is intentionally grounded is called the _____.
   a. grounding conductor
   b. neutral conductor
   c. grounded conductor
   d. Both b and c

3. Conductors other than _____ shall be protected against overcurrent, in accordance with their ampacities as specified in 310.15, unless otherwise permitted or required in 240.4(A) through (G).
   a. flexible cords
   b. flexible cables
   c. fixture wires
   d. All of the above

4. Article _____ contains the general requirements, installation requirements, and connection requirements for surge-protective devices (SPDS) permanently installed on premises' wiring systems of 1,000 volts or less.
   a. 240
   b. 250
   c. 280
   d. 285

5. The minimum size aluminum equipment grounding conductor for a circuit rated 100 amperes is _____ AWG.
   a. 8
   b. 6
   c. 4
   d. 2

6. For lampholders of the screw shell type that are supplied by circuits having a _____ conductor, this conductor shall be connected to the screw shell.
   a. grounded
   b. grounding
   c. ungrounded
   d. Either a or b

7. What is an acceptable means of providing overcurrent protection for a motor control circuit that is supplied from a 50 volt-ampere transformer that is an integral part of the motor controller and located within the motor controller enclosure?
   a. by the primary overcurrent device
   b. by an impedance limiting means
   c. by other inherent protective means
   d. All of the above

8. A 2 in. trade size intermediate metal conduit (IMC) has a metric designator of _____.
   a. 51
   b. 52
   c. 53
   d. 54

9. Where subject to physical damage, which of the following is not required to be protected?
   a. conductors
   b. equipment
   c. raceways
   d. cables

10. The provisions for ground-fault circuit-interrupter protection for feeders supplying 15- and 20-ampere receptacle branch circuits can be found in Section _____.
   a. 210.8
   b. 210.12
   c. 215.9
   d. 590.6(A)

11. Luminaires that are installed in a Class II, Division 1 location shall be protected against physical damage by _____.
   a. a suitable guard
   b. location
   c. a or **b**
   d. a and **b**

12. The use of a multi-outlet assembly shall be permitted _____.
   a. in dry locations
   b. in wet locations
   c. in damp locations
   d. where needed

13. Single-phase cord- and plug- connected room air conditioners shall be provided with which of the following factory-installed devices?
   a. leakage-current detector-interruptor (LCDI)
   b. arc-fault circuit interrupter (AFCI)
   c. heat detecting circuit interrupter (HDCI)
   d. a or **b** or **c**

14. For a branch circuit having two outlets and supplied by a 40 ampere overcurrent device, what is/are the permissible receptacle rating(s)?
   a. 30 A
   b. 40 A
   c. 50 A
   d. b and **c**

15. Nameplates or _____ shall provide the following information for all stationary generators and portable generators rated more than 15 kW:
   (1) Subtransient, transient, synchronous, and zero sequence reactances
   (2) Power rating category
   (3) Insulation system class
   (4) Indication if the generator is protected against overload by inherent design, an overcurrent protective relay, circuit breaker, or fuse
   (5) Maximum short-circuit current for inverter-based generators, in lieu of the synchronous, subtransient, and transient reactances
   a. the authority having jurisdiction
   b. blueprints
   c. manufacturer's instructions
   d. specifications

16. Storage batteries used as a source of power for emergency systems shall be of suitable rating and capacity to supply and maintain the total load for a minimum period of _____ hours, without the voltage applied to the load falling below $87\frac{1}{2}$ percent of normal.
   a. 1
   b. $1\frac{1}{2}$
   c. 2
   d. $2\frac{1}{2}$

17. The requirements for the installation of underground service conductors can be found in Part _____ of Article 230 – Services.
   a. I
   b. II
   c. III
   d. IV

18. Which of the following symbols that are commonly found on plans and prints represents a lighting outlet?

a.

b.

c.

d.

19. What is the allowable ampacity for a 1/0 aluminum conductor, type TW, installed in a raceway with 2 other current carrying conductors?
 a. 85 amperes
 b. 100 amperes
 c. 120 amperes
 d. 125 amperes

20. The grounded circuit conductor for the controlled lighting circuit shall be installed at the location where switches control lighting loads that are supplied by a grounded general-purpose branch circuit serving bathrooms, hallways, stairways, or rooms suitable for human habitation. Which of the following is an exception to this requirement?
 a. where a switch controls a receptacle load
 b. where a switch controls a dining room lighting load
 c. where a switch controls a kitchen lighting load
 d. where a switch controls a bedroom lighting load

21. Where raceways are installed in wet locations above grade, the interior of these raceways shall be considered to be a _____ location.
 a. dry
 b. damp
 c. accessible
 d. wet

22. The definition of *controller*, as it pertains to motors, is any switch or device that is normally used to start and stop a motor by making and breaking the _____.
 a. motor disconnecting means
 b. motor overload circuit
 c. motor circuit current
 d. motor branch-circuit

23. An electrical appliance is rated at 5,000 watts and 240 volts. How much current will this appliance draw?
 a. 2.08 amperes
 b. 20.8 amperes
 c. 48 amperes
 d. 120 amperes

24. Which article applies to all permanently installed energy storage systems operating at over 50 volts AC or 60 volts DC that may be stand-alone or interactive with other electric power production sources?
 a. 690
 b. 691
 c. 705
 d. 706

25. Fuses and circuit breakers shall be permitted to be connected in parallel where they are factory assembled in parallel and listed as a unit. Which of the following shall not be connected in parallel?
a. individual fuses
b. individual circuit breakers
c. combinations of individual fuses and circuit breakers
d. All of the above

26. Ground-fault protection of equipment shall be provided for solidly grounded wye electrical systems of more than 150 volts to ground, but not exceeding 1,000 volts phase-to-phase for each individual device used as a building or structure main disconnecting means rated 1,000 amperes or more. What type of equipment is excluded from this rule?
a. emergency generators
b. fire pumps
c. egress lighting
d. de-icing and snow-melting equipment

27. A 10 hp 240 volt, DC motor has a full-load current of _____ amperes.
a. 38
b. 55
c. 72
d. 76

28. Locations of lamps for outdoor lighting shall be below _____.
a. transformers
b. all energized conductors
c. Neither **a.** or **b.**
d. Both **a.** and **b.**

29. For a metal box sized 4" × 4" × 4", the minimum thickness of the steel shall be _____.
a. 0.0625 inches
b. 0.078 inches
c. 0.625 inches
d. 1.59 inches

30. Where a branch circuit supplies continuous loads or any combination of continuous and noncontinuous loads, the rating of the overcurrent device shall not be less than _____ percent of the noncontinuous load plus _____ percent of the continuous load.
a. 80, 100
b. 100, 100
c. 100, 125
d. 80, 125

31. For swimming pool underwater lighting, what is the maximum voltage between conductors?
a. 115 volts
b. 125 volts
c. 150 volts
d. 240 volts

32. What is the minimum distance that an adequately supported, mast-type, 120/240 volt service, can extend above a roof?
a. 18 inches
b. 48 inches
c. 6 feet
d. 8 feet

33. According to Ohm's Law, $I^2 \times R$ is the formula for _____.
a. voltage
b. power
c. resistance
d. amperage

34. The uses permitted for flat cable assemblies include all but _____.
  a. as branch circuits to supply suitable tap devices for lighting, small appliances, or small power loads. The rating of the branch circuit shall not exceed 30 amperes
  b. where exposed to corrosive conditions, unless suitable for the application
  c. in locations where they will not be subjected to physical damage
  d. where installed for exposed work

35. For conductors installed in a raceway, what is the maximum size that may be solid?
  a. 14 AWG
  b. 12 AWG
  c. 10 AWG
  d. 8 AWG

36. For a grounded system, an unspliced _____ shall be used to connect the equipment grounding conductor(s) and the service-disconnect enclosure to the grounded conductor within the enclosure for each service disconnect.
  a. system bonding jumper
  b. supply-side bonding jumper
  c. equipment bonding jumper
  d. main bonding jumper

37. Which of the following pieces of equipment do not require dedicated space?
  a. transfer switches
  b. switchgear
  c. panelboard
  d. motor control centers

38. Type _____ cable shall have an armor of flexible metal tape and shall have an internal bonding strip of copper or aluminum in intimate contact with the armor for its entire length.
  a. MC
  b. AC
  c. NM
  d. MI

39. A box or conduit body shall be installed at each conductor splice point, outlet point, switch point, junction point, termination point, or pull point, unless otherwise permitted. Which wiring method is the exception to this requirement?
  a. knob-and-tube wiring
  b. non-metallic sheathed cable
  c. metal-clad cable
  d. mineral-insulated cable

40. Class _____ circuits shall be installed in accordance with Part I of Article 300 and with the wiring methods from the appropriate articles in Chapter 3.
  a. 3
  b. 2
  c. 1
  d. All of the above

41. An insulating bushing or "red-head" shall be provided at all termination points, between the conductors and the armor of which cable type(s)?
  a. MC
  b. AC
  c. NM
  d. Both **a** and **b**

42. The volume of non-metallic boxes, 100 in.³ or less, shall be determined by:
  a. Table 314.16(A)
  b. Table 314.16(B)
  c. manufacturers marking
  d. All of the above

43. Section 110.26 provides the requirements for working spaces about electrical equipment. Table 110.26(A)(1) provides the specific details for the minimum _____ clearances for equipment under specific conditions.
  a. height
  b. width
  c. volume
  d. depth

44. In dwelling unit's branch-circuits, the voltage shall not exceed _____ volts, nominal, between conductors that supply the terminals of luminaires.
  a. 120
  b. 125
  c. 240
  d. 250

45. Calculate the minimum number of 15A, lighting branch circuits, for a 2,440 ft.² dwelling unit.
  a. 4
  b. 4.06
  c. 5
  d. 6

46. Nonmetallic-sheathed cable is to be run through bored holes in the wooden framing members of a dwelling unit. The edge of the hole shall not be less than _____ in. from the nearest edge of the wood member.
  a. $\frac{3}{4}$
  b. 1
  c. $1\frac{1}{4}$
  d. 2

47. A _____ is intended to protect the motors against dangerous overheating due to overload and failure to start.
  a. circuit breaker
  b. thermal protector
  c. motor circuit switch
  d. surge-protective device

48. For straight runs of $1\frac{1}{2}$ in. rigid metal conduit, the maximum distance between supports shall be _____ ft.
  a. 10
  b. 14
  c. 16
  d. 20

49. Where a metal lampholder is attached to a flexible cord, the inlet shall be equipped with an insulating bushing that, if threaded, is not smaller than a _____ in. pipe size.
  a. $\frac{1}{2}$
  b. $\frac{1}{4}$
  c. $\frac{3}{8}$
  d. $\frac{5}{8}$

50. The provisions for the disconnecting means for fixed outdoor snow-melting equipment can be found in Article/Section _____.
a. 422 Part III
b. 517.17(C)
c. 427.55
d. 426.50 (A)

51. For a given conductor size, which of the following material provides the greatest ampacity?
a. copper
b. aluminum
c. copper-clad aluminum
d. Both **b** and **c**

52. Low voltage at an appliance (high voltage drop) in a home can be caused by _____.
a. poor connections at the terminals
b. a circuit that is too long
c. a conductor that is too small for the load
d. All of the above

53. Feeder conductors shall have an ampacity not less than required to supply the load, and shall be sized as follows:
a. Where a feeder supplies continuous loads or any combination of continuous and noncontinuous loads, the minimum feeder conductor size shall have an allowable ampacity not less than the noncontinuous load plus 125 percent of the continuous load.
b. The minimum feeder conductor size shall have an allowable ampacity not less than the maximum load to be served after the application of any adjustment or correction factors.
c. The minimum feeder conductor shall be sized to carry not less than the larger of **a** or **b**.
d. Both **a** and **b** must be applied if both conditions exist.

54. For the purpose of calculating branch circuits, all of the following are considered nominal system voltages except _____.
a. 120
b. 125/250
c. 208Y/120
d. 480Y/277

55. This code is divided into the introduction and nine chapters. Chapters 1, 2, 3, and 4 apply generally. Chapter _____ may supplement or modify the requirements in Chapters 1 through 7.
a. 5
b. 6
c. 7
d. All of the above

56. In a marina, electrical connections shall be located at least _____ in. above the deck of a floating pier.
   a. 12
   b. 24
   c. 36
   d. 60

57. Where the number of current-carrying conductors in a raceway is nine, the individual ampacity of each conductor shall be reduced by _____.
   a. 70% due to the number of conductors
   b. 80% due to the number of conductors
   c. 80% if the conductors supply continuous loads
   d. Both **a** and **b**

58. An electrician would reference Table _____ to obtain the allowable ampacity for flexible cords and cables.
   a. 310.15(B)(16)
   b. 400.4
   c. 400.5(A)(1)
   d. 400.5(A)(2)

59. A motor controller shall be marked with a short-circuit current rating, except where _____.
   a. the short-circuit current rating is marked elsewhere on the assembly
   b. the controller is rated for a 480V, 3 hp motor
   c. Both **a** and **b**
   d. Neither **a** nor **b**

60. Bends in Type MC cable shall be so made that the cable will not be damaged. The radius of the curve of the inner edge of any bend shall not be less than _____ times the external diameter of the sheath for interlocked-type armor.
   a. 4
   b. 5
   c. 7
   d. 9

61. An overload is a condition caused by _____.
   a. an ungrounded conductor, unintentionally coming into contact with a grounded conductor
   b. operation of equipment in excess of normal, full-load rating
   c. an ungrounded conductor, unintentionally coming into contact with a grounded surface
   d. all of the above

62. A junction box size of _____ is the smallest allowed for the following installation: 2" EMT containing 4 – 1/0 AWG conductors, tubing to enter adjacent sides of box (see diagram).

   a. 10" × 10"
   b. 12" × 12"
   c. 14" × 14"
   d. 12" × 10"

63. Grounding electrode conductors shall be bonded to the grounding electrode by means of _____.
   a. listed pressure connectors
   b. exothermic welding
   c. soldering
   d. Either **a** or **b**

64. Conductors, not specifically permitted elsewhere in the NEC to be covered or bare, shall be _____.
a. supported
b. listed
c. insulated
d. permitted

65. Nonmetallic-sheathed cable shall be supported within _____ of a metal box.
a. 8 in.
b. 12 in.
c. 4 ft.
d. $4\frac{1}{2}$ ft.

66. Thermal insulation shall not be installed within _____ in. of a non-type IC rated recessed luminaire.
a. $\frac{1}{2}$
b. 3
c. 5
d. 6

67. Flexible metallic tubing shall not be used _____.
a. in lengths over 6 ft.
b. in dry locations
c. in accessible locations
d. where concealed

68. Intrinsically safe apparatus, associated apparatus, and other equipment shall be installed in accordance with the _____.
a. authority having jurisdiction
b. insurance company
c. architect's designs
d. control drawings

69. What is the purpose of equipotential bonding in swimming pools?
a. to provide an adequate ground-fault current path
b. to facilitate the operation of the over-current protection device
c. to reduce voltage gradients in the pool area
d. All of the above

70. An 8 AWG grounded conductor shall be identified by _____.
a. a distinctive white marking at its terminations
b. stripping the insulation off and leaving it bare
c. a continuous white outer finish
d. a continuous green outer finish

71. Electrical equipment that is likely to require examination, adjustment, servicing, or maintenance while energized shall be field or factory marked to warn qualified persons of potential electric arc flash hazards. This provision does not apply to _____.
a. commercial panelboards
b. residential panelboards
c. industrial control centers
d. meter socket enclosures

72. A 125-volt, 15-amp receptacle is installed outdoors to provide dedicated power for electric snow-melting equipment. This outlet is _____.
a. required to have GFCI protection
b. required to be readily accessible
c. not required to have GFCI protection
d. required to have AFCI protection

73. Each meeting room of not more than 1,000 ft², in other than dwelling units, shall have outlets for nonlocking-type, 125-volt, 15- or 20-ampere receptacles installed, such that no point measured horizontally along the floor line is more than _____ ft. from a receptacle.
a. 4
b. 6
c. 10
d. 12

74. A main bonding jumper and a system bonding jumper shall be any of the following except a _____.
a. connector
b. wire
c. bus
d. screw

75. Final spans for feeders, to the buildings they supply, or from which they are fed, shall be permitted to be attached to the building, but they shall be kept not less than _____ from windows that are designed to be opened, and from doors, porches, balconies, ladders, stairs, fire escapes, or similar locations
a. 18 in.
b. 24 in.
c. 36 in.
d. 48 in.

76. A disconnecting means for a piece of equipment is located above a drop ceiling. This equipment is likely to require examination, adjustment, servicing, or maintenance while energized. The access opening for this installation shall not be smaller than _____.
a. 18" × 18"
b. 20" × 20"
c. 22" × 30"
d. 22" × 22"

77. PV system DC circuits on or in one- and two-family dwellings shall be permitted to have a maximum voltage of _____ volts or less.
a. 240
b. 480
c. 600
d. 1,000

78. A unit of an electrical system that carries or controls electrical energy as its principal function is a _____.
a. utilization equipment
b. circuit breaker
c. switch
d. device

79. A transformer operates on the principle of _____.
a. Watt's Law
b. mutual inductance
c. Kirchhoff's Law
d. Thevenin's theorem

80. Unused openings for _____ and switches shall be closed using identified closures, or other approved means that provide protection substantially equivalent to the wall of the enclosure.
a. circuit breakers
b. receptacles
c. panelboards
d. knockouts

Answers and Explanations

1. The correct answer is **c**. Mandatory rules of the NEC are those that identify actions that are required or prohibited, and are characterized by the use of the terms *shall* and *shall not*. Choice **a** is incorrect because enforceable is not a type of rule within the National Electrical Code. The term *enforcement* is used to indicate that governmental bodies, such as an authority having jurisdiction, have an obligation to require that the rules of the NEC are followed. Choice **b** is incorrect because permissive rules are those that are allowed but not required. Choice **d** is incorrect because there are no explanatory rules within the NEC. There may be explanatory material included in various articles in the form of Information Notes. This information is not enforceable as requirements of the NEC. (NEC 90.5(A))

2. The correct answer is **c**. The grounded conductor is a system or circuit conductor that is intentionally grounded. Choice **a** is incorrect because the grounding conductor provides a ground-fault current path and connects normally non-current-carrying metal parts of equipment together and to the system grounded conductor or to the grounding electrode conductor, or both. Choice **b** is incorrect because the neutral conductor is connected to the neutral point of a system that is intended to carry current under normal conditions. This connection is made to ground, thus potentially making this conductor a grounded conductor. However, not all grounded conductors are used in this fashion and therefore they are not all neutral conductors. Choice **d** is incorrect because the neutral conductor is connected to the neutral point of a system that is intended to carry current under normal conditions. This connection is made to ground, thus potentially making this conductor a grounded conductor. However, not all grounded conductors are used in this fashion and therefore they are not all neutral conductors. (NEC 100)

3. The correct answer is **d**. Flexible cords, flexible cables, and fixture wires are all listed as conductors that are not required to be protected in accordance with their ampacities. Choice **a** is incorrect because flexible cords are one of three of the exceptions listed as conductors that are not required to be protected in accordance with their ampacities. Choice **b** is incorrect because flexible cables are one of three exceptions listed as conductors that are not required to be protected in accordance with their ampacities. Choice **c** is incorrect because fixture wires are one of three exceptions listed as conductors that are not required to be protected in accordance with their ampacities. (NEC 240.4)

4. The correct answer is **d**. Article 285 contains requirements pertaining to surge-protectice devices permanently installed on premises wiring systems of 1,000 volts or less. Choice **a** is incorrect because Article 240 contains requirements pertaining to overcurrent protections. Choice **b** is incorrect because Article 250 contains requirements pertaining to grounding and bonding. Choice **c** is incorrect because Article 280 contains requirements pertaining to surge arrestors over 1,000 volts. (NEC 285)

5. The correct answer is **b**. A 6 AWG aluminum grounding conductor is sufficient for a 100 ampere circuit. Choice **a** is incorrect because an 8 AWG aluminum grounding conductor is insufficient for a 100 ampere circuit. Choice **c** is incorrect because a 4 AWG aluminum grounding conductor is sufficient for a 200 ampere circuit. Choice **d** is incorrect because a 2 AWG aluminum grounding conductor is sufficient for a 300 ampere circuit. (NEC Table 250.122)

6. The correct answer is **a**. For lampholders of the screw shell type that are supplied by circuits having a grounded conductor, this conductor shall be connected to the screw shell. Choice **b** is incorrect because the screw shell of the lampholder is a current carrying component. If the grounding conductor were connected to it, the lampholder would operate but with a hazardous current being placed on the grounding system of the circuit. Choice **c** is incorrect because the screw shell of the lampholder is a current carrying component. It is also the part of the lampholder where the lamp is screwed in. If the lampholder were installed with reverse polarity, the ungrounded conductor would be connected to the screw shell. This would create a touch hazard to anyone attempting to replace a burned out lamp. Choice **d** is incorrect because if the grounding conductor were connected to it, the lampholder would operate but with a hazardous current being placed on the grounding system of the circuit. (NEC 410.90)

7. The correct answer is **d**. Overcurrent protections for the motor control circuit described can be provided by the primary overcurrent device, impedance limiting means, or other inherent protective means. Choice **a** is incorrect because overcurrent protections for the motor control circuit described can be provided by the primary overcurrent device. However, this is just one of three acceptable methods. Choice **b** is incorrect because overcurrent protections for the motor control circuit described can be provided by an impedance limiting means. However, this is just one of three acceptable methods. Choice **c** is incorrect because overcurrent protections for the motor control circuit described can be provided by other inherent protective means. However, this is just one of three acceptable methods. (NEC 430.72(C)(3))

8. The correct answer is **c**. While Article 344 provides details on IMC and the minimum and maximum trade sizes permitted, it does not actually give the entire scope of trade sizes and their metric equivalent. Section 300.1(C) provides a detailed reference to all sizes of conduit, tubing, and associated fittings. The correct answer is 53. Choices **a**, **b**, and **d** are incorrect. (NEC Table 300.1(C))

9. The correct answer is **b**. Equipment is not one of the three items listed that requires protections from physical damage in Article 300, which states the requirements for wiring methods and materials. Choice **a** is incorrect because conductors are one of the three items listed that requires protections from physical damage. Choice **c** is incorrect because raceways are one of the three items listed that requires protections from physical damage. Choice **d** is incorrect because cables are one of the three items listed that requires protections from physical damage. (NEC 300.4)

10. The correct answer is **c**. Section 215.9 provides the provisions for ground-fault circuit-interrupter protection for feeders supplying 15- and 20-ampere receptacle branch circuits. Choice **a** is incorrect because Section 210.8 provides the provisions for ground-fault circuit-interrupter protection for branch circuits. Choice **b** is incorrect because Section 210.12 provides the provisions for arc-fault circuit-interrupter protection for branch circuits. Choice **d** is incorrect because Section 590.6(A) provides the provisions for ground-fault circuit-interrupter

protection for temporary wiring installations. (NEC 215.9)

11. The correct answer is **c**. Luminaires that are installed in a Class II, Division 1 location shall be protected against physical damage by a suitable guard *or* by location. Choice **a** is incorrect because a suitable guard is one of the two correct answers, the other being by location. Choice **b** is incorrect because location is one of the two correct answers, the other being by a suitable guard. Choice **d** is incorrect because luminaires that are installed in a Class II, Division 1 location shall be protected against physical damage by a suitable guard *or* by location. (NEC 502.130(A)(2))

12. The correct answer is **a**. The use of a multi-outlet assembly shall be permitted in dry locations. Choice **b** is incorrect because the use of a multi-outlet assembly shall be permitted in dry locations only as they are not constructed to withstand water. Choice **c** is incorrect because the use of a multi-outlet assembly shall be permitted in dry locations only; they are not constructed to withstand moisture. Choice **d** is incorrect because the use of a multi-outlet assembly shall not be permitted to be installed where needed, but only in a location suitable for their construction. (NEC 380.10)

13. The correct answer is **d**. Single-phase cord- and plug-connected room air conditioners shall be provided with any of the following factory-installed devices: leakage-current detector-interruptor (LCDI) or arc-fault circuit interrupter (AFCI) or heat detecting circuit interrupter (HDCI). Choice **a** is incorrect because a leakage-current detector-interruptor (LCDI) is one of three acceptable protective devices for single-phase cord- and plug-connected room air conditioners. Choice **b** is incorrect because an arc-fault circuit interrupter (AFCI) is one of three acceptable protective devices for single-phase cord- and plug-connected room air conditioners. Choice **c** is incorrect because a heat detecting circuit interrupter (HDCI) is one of three acceptable protective devices for single-phase cord- and plug-connected room air conditioners. (NEC 440.65)

14. The correct answer is **d**. Receptacles rated either 40 or 50 A are permissible on a 40 ampere branch circuit serving two outlets. Choice **a** is incorrect because a receptacle rated 30 A is not permissible on a 40 ampere branch circuit. Choice **b** is incorrect because a receptacle rated 40 A is one of two ratings permissible on a 40 ampere branch circuit. Choice **c** is incorrect because a receptacle rated 50 A is one of two ratings permissible on a 40 ampere branch circuit. (NEC Table 210.24)

15. The correct answer is **c**. Nameplates or manufacturer's instructions shall provide the specific electrical characteristics for all stationary generators and portable generators rated more than 15 kW. Choice **a** is incorrect because the authority having jurisdiction's job is to approve equipment, and not to require any listing specifics. Choice **b** is incorrect because blueprints provide information for the installation of electrical equipment and the systems and circuits required to run them. Choice **d** is incorrect because specifications accompany blueprints and provide additional and more specific information for the installation of electrical equipment and the systems and circuits required to run them. (NEC 445.11)

16. The correct answer is **b**. Storage batteries used as a source of power for emergency systems shall be of suitable rating and capacity to supply and maintain the total load for a minimum period of $1\frac{1}{2}$ hours, without the voltage applied to the load falling below $87\frac{1}{2}$ percent of normal. Choices **a**, **c**, and **d** are incorrect. (NEC 700.12(A))

17. The correct answer is **c**. Part III of Article 230 provides the requirements for the installation of underground service conductors for services. Choice **a** is incorrect because Part I of Article 230 provides general information with regard to services. Choice **b** is incorrect because Part II of Article 230 provides information with regard to overhead service conductors for services. Choice **d** is incorrect because Part IV of Article 230 provides information with regard to service-entrance conductors for services. (NEC 230 Part III)

18. The correct answer is **a**. This is the symbol for a lighting outlet. Choice **b** is incorrect because it is the symbol for ground. Choice **c** is incorrect because it is the symbol for a duplex receptacle. Choice **d** is incorrect because it is the symbol for a battery.

19. The correct answer is **b**. 100 amperes is the allowable ampacity for a 1/0 AWG aluminum conductor, type TW. Choice **a** is incorrect because 85 amperes is the allowable ampacity for a 1 AWG aluminum conductor, type TW. Choice **c** is incorrect because 120 amperes is the allowable ampacity for a 1/0 AWG aluminum conductor, type THW. Choice **d** is incorrect because 125 amperes is the allowable ampacity for a 1 AWG copper conductor, type TW. (NEC Table 310.15(B)(16))

20. The correct answer is **a**. Where a switch controls a receptacle load is listed as one of the exceptions to the requirement. Choice **b** is incorrect because a grounded circuit conductor is required at the location of a switch controlling a dining room lighting load as it would be considered a habitable room. Choice **c** is incorrect because a grounded circuit conductor is required at the location of a switch controlling a kitchen lighting load as it would be considered a habitable room. Choice **d** is incorrect because a grounded circuit conductor is required at the location of a switch controlling a bedroom lighting load as it would be considered a habitable room. (NEC 404.2(C))

21. The correct answer is **d**. The interior of raceways installed in wet locations above grade cannot be kept dry in all environments. Therefore, it is considered to be a wet location and all conductors and cables installed in the raceways must be suitable for the location. Choice **a** is incorrect because the interior of raceways installed in wet locations above grade cannot be kept dry in all environments. Therefore, it is considered to be a wet location and all conductors and cables installed in the raceways must be suitable for the location. Choice **b** is incorrect because the interior of raceways installed in wet locations above grade cannot be kept free from moisture in all environments. Therefore, it is considered to be a wet location and all conductors and cables installed in the raceways must be suitable for the location. Choice **c** is incorrect because accessibility does not pertain to whether a location is considered wet, dry, or damp. (NEC 300.9)

22. The correct answer is **c**. The motor circuit current is made and broken in order to start and stop a motor. Choice **a** is incorrect because a motor disconnecting means may be considered a controller, but it is the motor circuit current that is being made and broken in order to start and stop the motor. Choice **b** is incorrect because a motor overload circuit is the part of the system that protects the motor from damage caused by excessive current. It is the motor circuit current that is being made and broken in order to start and stop the motor under normal running conditions. Choice **d** is incorrect because a motor branch-circuit is the system that provides electrical power to the motor. However, it is the motor circuit current that is being made and broken in order to start and stop the motor. (NEC 430.2)

23. The correct answer is **b**. The answer can be determined by applying the correct Watt's Law formula of $I = P \div E$, where I = current in amperes, P = power in watts, and E = voltage in volts. The correct answer is determined as follows: 5,000 watts ÷ 240 volts = 20.8 amperes. Choices **a**, **c**, and **d** are incorrect. (Watt's Law)

24. The correct answer is **d**. Article 706 applies to all permanently installed energy storage systems operating at over 50 volts AC or 60 volts DC that may be stand-alone or interactive with other electric power production sources. Choice **a** is incorrect because Article 690 applies to solar photovoltaic (PV) systems. Article 706 applies to all permanently installed energy storage systems operating at over 50 volts AC or 60 volts DC that may be stand-alone or interactive with other electric power production sources. Choice **b** is incorrect because Article 691 applies to large-scale photovoltaic (PV) electric power production facilities. Article 706 applies to all permanently installed energy storage systems operating at over 50 volts AC or 60 volts DC that may be stand-alone or interactive with other electric power production sources. Choice **c** is incorrect because Article 705 applies to interconnected electric power production sources. Article 706 applies to all permanently installed energy storage systems operating at over 50 volts AC or 60 volts DC that may be stand-alone or interactive with other electric power production sources. (NEC 706)

25. The correct answer is **d**. Individual fuses, circuit breakers, or combinations thereof shall not otherwise be connected in parallel. Choice **a** is incorrect because individual fuses shall not be connected in parallel, but this is just one of three conditions listed. Choice **b** is incorrect because individual circuit breakers shall not be connected in parallel but this is just one of three conditions listed. Choice **c** is incorrect because combinations of individual fuses and circuit breakers shall not be connected in parallel but this is just one of three conditions listed. (NEC 240.8)

26. The correct answer is **b**. Fire pumps that are supplied by a solidly grounded wye electrical system of more than 150 volts to ground but not exceeding 1,000 volts phase-to-phase shall not be provided with ground-fault protections. Choice **a** is incorrect because it is required that emergency generators shall be provided with ground-fault protection if they are solidly grounded wye electrical systems of more than 150 volts to ground but not exceeding 1,000 volts phase-to-phase. Choice **c** is incorrect because it would be unusual for egress lighting to be supplied by a solidly grounded wye electrical system of more than 150 volts to ground, but not exceeding 1,000 volts phase-to-phase, but if it were, it would require ground-fault protection. Choice **d** is incorrect because it would be unusual for de-icing and snow-melting equipment to be supplied by a solidly grounded wye electrical system of more than 150 volts to ground but not exceeding 1,000 volts phase-to-phase, but if it were, it would require ground-fault protection. (NEC 240.13)

27. The correct answer is **a**. According to Table 430.247, a 10 hp, 240 volt, DC motor has a full-load current of 38 amperes. Choices **b**, **c**, and **d** are incorrect. (NEC Table 430.247)

28. The correct answer is **d**. Outdoor lighting lamps shall be below all energized conductors and transformers. Choice **a** is incorrect because outdoor lighting lamps shall be below transformers, but this is not the only applicable location listed. Choice **b** is incorrect because outdoor lighting lamps shall be below all energized conductors, but this is not the only applicable location listed. Choice **c** is incorrect because outdoor lighting lamps shall be below all energized conductors and transformers. (NEC 225.25)

29. The correct answer is **a**. Sheet steel boxes not over 100 inches^3 in size shall be made from steel not less than 0.0625 inches thick. The box described has a volume of 64 inches^3. Choice **b** is incorrect because steel thickness of 0.078 inches is more than required by the NEC. Choice **c** is incorrect because steel thickness of 0.625 inches is more than required by the NEC. Choice **d** is incorrect because steel thickness of 1.59 inches is much more than is reasonable and required by the NEC. (NEC 314.40(B))

30. The correct answer is **c**. Where a branch circuit supplies continuous loads or any combination of continuous and noncontinuous loads, the rating of the overcurrent device shall not be less than the noncontinuous load plus 125 percent of the continuous load. Choice **a** is incorrect because the ratings of branch circuits shall be sufficient to carry the load and not exceed the limitations of the conductors and devices. 80 percent of the noncontinuous and 100 percent of the continuous load could lead to an overload condition. Choice **b** is incorrect because 100 percent of the noncontinuous and 100 percent of the continuous load could lead to an overload condition. Choice **d** is incorrect because 80 percent of the noncontinuous and 125 percent of the continuous load could lead to an overload condition. (NEC 210.20(A))

31. The correct answer is **c**. No luminaires shall be installed for operation on supply circuits over 150 volts between conductors. Choice **a** is incorrect because 115 volts between conductors feeding underwater swimming pool lighting is within the requirements of the NEC. However, it is not the maximum voltage allowed. Choice **b** is incorrect because 125 volts between conductors feeding underwater swimming pool lighting is within the requirements of the NEC. However, it is not the maximum voltage allowed. Choice **d** is incorrect because 240 volts between conductors feeding underwater swimming pool lighting exceeds the requirements of the NEC. (NEC 680.23(A)(4))

32. The correct answer is **a**. According to Section 240.24(A), conductors shall have a vertical clearance of not less than 8 feet above roof surfaces. However, an adequately supported, mast-type, 120/240 volt service meets the conditions of Exception No. 3, which allows a minimum clearance of 18 inches. Choice **b** is incorrect because 48 inches exceeds the minimum distance allowed, which is 18 inches. Choice **c** is incorrect because 6 feet exceeds the minimum distance allowed, which is 18 inches. Choice **d** is incorrect because 8 feet exceeds the minimum distance allowed, which is 18 inches. (NEC 230.24(A) *Exception No. 3*)

33. The correct answer is **b**. According to Ohm's Law, $I^2 \times R$ is the formula for power. Choice **a** is incorrect because according to Ohm's Law, $I \times R$ is the formula for voltage. Choice **c** is incorrect because according to Ohm's Law, $E \times I$ is one of the formulas for resistance. Choice **d** is incorrect because according to Ohm's Law, $E \times R$ is one of the formulas for amperage. (Ohm's Law)

34. The correct answer is **b**. Flat cable assemblies shall not be used where exposed to corrosive conditions, unless suitable for the application. Choice **a** is incorrect because according to Section 322.10(1), flat cable assemblies shall be permitted as branch circuits to supply suitable tap devices for lighting, small appliances, or small power loads. The rating of the branch circuit shall not exceed 30 amperes. Choice **c** is incorrect because according to Section 322.10(3), flat cable assemblies shall be permitted in locations where they will not be subjected to physical damage. Choice **d** is incorrect because according to Section 322.10(2), flat cable assemblies shall be permitted where installed for exposed work. (NEC 322.12(1))

35. The correct answer is **c**. 10 AWG solid conductors may be installed in raceways and they are the maximum size. Choice **a** is incorrect because 14 AWG solid conductors may be installed in raceways but they are not the maximum size. Choice **b** is incorrect because 12 AWG solid conductors may be installed in raceways but they are not the maximum size. Choice **d** is incorrect because 8 AWG solid conductors may not be installed in raceways. Because 8 AWG solid conductors are not very pliable, the conductors could be damaged while being installed into the raceways. (NEC 310.106(C))

36. The correct answer is **d**. For a grounded system, an unspliced main bonding jumper shall be used to connect the equipment grounding conductor(s) and the service-disconnect enclosure to the grounded conductor within the enclosure for each service disconnect. Choice **a** is incorrect because the system bonding jumper is used to connect the grounded circuit conductor to the equipment grounding conductor at a separately derived system. Choice **b** is incorrect because a supply-side bonding jumper is a conductor installed on the supply side of a service or within a service equipment enclosure(s), or for a separately derived system, that ensures the required electrical conductivity between metal parts required to be electrically connected. Choice **c** is incorrect because the equipment bonding jumper is the connection between two or more portions of the equipment grounding conductor. (NEC 250.24(B))

37. The correct answer is **a**. Transfer switches are not listed among the equipment that shall be located in dedicated space and protected from damage. The equipment listed is: all switchboards, switchgear, panelboards, and motor control centers. Choices **b**, **c**, and **d** are incorrect because all switchboards, switchgear, panelboards, and motor control centers shall be located in dedicated spaces and protected from damage. (NEC 110.26(E))

38. The correct answer is **b**. Type AC (armored) cable shall have an armor of flexible metal tape and shall have an internal bonding strip of copper or aluminum in intimate contact with the armor for its entire length. Choice **a** is incorrect because Type MC (metal-clad) cable may be constructed of interlocking metal tape armor, but it does not have an internal bonding strip of copper or aluminum. Choice **c** is incorrect because Type NM (non-metallic sheathed) cable is a factory assembly of two or more insulated conductors enclosed within an overall nonmetallic jacket. Choice **d** is incorrect because Type MI (mineral-insulated, metal-sheathed) cable is a factory assembly of one or more conductors insulated with a compressed refractory mineral insulation and enclosed in a liquid-tight and gas-tight continuous copper or alloy steel sheath (NEC 320.100)

39. The correct answer is **a**. Knob-and-tube wiring is an outdated wiring method that allowed circuit conductors to be run separately along building framing members. Conductors were openly spliced, with rubber and cloth tape as protection against short-circuits. It was therefore impractical to install a box at each splice location. Choices **b**, **c**, and **d** are incorrect because where the wiring method is conduit, tubing, Type AC cable, Type MC cable, Type MI cable, nonmetallic-sheathed cable, or other cables, a box or conduit body shall be installed at each conductor splice point, outlet point, switch point, junction point, termination point, or pull point, unless otherwise permitted. (NEC 300.15)

40. The correct answer is **c**. Class 1 circuits are the portion of the wiring system between the load side of the overcurrent device or power-limited supply and the connected equipment. They therefore may be of higher voltages and currents and shall be installed in accordance with Part I of Article 300 and with the wiring methods from the appropriate articles in Chapter 3. Choice **a** is incorrect because Class 3 circuits are considered to be power-limited according to article 725. Therefore, they may or may not need to conform to the wiring methods set forth in Part I of Article 300 and with the wiring methods from the appropriate articles in Chapter 3. Choice **b** is incorrect because Class 2 circuits are considered to be power-limited according to article 725. Therefore, they may or may not need to conform to the wiring methods set forth in Part I of Article 300 and with the wiring methods from the appropriate articles in Chapter 3. Choice **d** is incorrect because only Class 1 circuits shall be installed in accordance with Part I of Article 300 and with the wiring methods from the appropriate articles in Chapter 3. (NEC 725.46)

41. The correct answer is **b**. An insulating bushing or "red-head" shall be provided at all termination points, between the conductors and the armor, for type AC cable. Choice **a** is incorrect because the NEC does not require insulating bushing at the termination points for type MC cable. However, the manufacturer suggests that it is a good practice to install one. Choice **c** is incorrect because Type NM is a non-metallic sheathed cable, and therefore it is not necessary to provide insulating bushing. Choice **d** is incorrect because the NEC does not require insulating bushing at the termination points for type MC cable. (NEC 320.40)

42. The correct answer is **c**. Nonmetallic boxes shall be durably and legibly marked by the manufacturer with their volumes. Choice **a** is incorrect because Table 314.16(A) provides the volume for metal boxes only. Choice **b** is incorrect because Table 314.16(B) provides the volume allowance required per conductor. Choice **d** is incorrect because only nonmetallic boxes shall be durably and legibly marked by the manufacturer with their volumes. The volume of metal boxes shall be provided in Table 314.16(A). (NEC 314.16(A)(2))

43. The correct answer is **d**. The depth of the working space about electrical equipment shall not be less than that specified in Table 110.26(A)(1). Choice **a** is incorrect because the height of working space is provided in Section 110.26(A)(3). Choice **b** is incorrect because the width of working space is provided in Section 110.26(A)(2). Choice **c** is incorrect because there is no volume, as the question pertains to working clearances about electrical equipment. (NEC 110.26(A)(1))

44. The correct answer is **a**. In dwelling units, the voltage shall not exceed 120 volts, nominal, between conductors that supply the terminals of luminaires. Choice **b** is incorrect because the value of 125 volts is that which is used in the rating of devices. Choice **c** is incorrect because the value of 240 volts is considered an unsafe voltage for the average person to come in contact with. Therefore, the maximum voltage is listed as 120 volts. Choice **d** is incorrect because the value of 250 volts is considered an unsafe voltage for the average person to come in contact with. Therefore, the maximum voltage is listed as 120 volts. (NEC 210.6(A))

45. The correct answer is **c**. To solve, you must first calculate the total load in volt-amperes. According to Section 220.12, this is accomplished by multiplying the total area of the dwelling unit by the unit loads, based on occupancy, listed in Table 220.12. For this dwelling, that calculation would be: 2,440 ft.^{2} × 3 volt-amperes/ft.^{2} (VA/ft.^{2}) = 7,320 volt-amperes (VA). Branch circuits according to amperes, not volt-amperes. So the total load in amperes must be determined using Ohm's Law. The formula is I = P ÷ E. Therefore, the total load in amperes = 7,320 VA ÷ 120 V = 61 A. The last step is to determine the minimum number of 15A branch circuits needed to carry this load. Therefore, 61 A ÷ 15 A = 4.06 circuits. Since it is impossible to run a fraction of a circuit, if the answer is not a whole number, you must always round up to the nearest whole number. A minimum of five 15-ampere branch circuits are required to satisfy the lighting load in this dwelling unit. Choice **a** is incorrect because four circuits do not meet the minimum requirement. Choice **b** is incorrect because 4.06 circuits do not meet the minimum requirement and it is impossible to run a fraction of a circuit. Choice **d** is incorrect because six circuits would be sufficient to carry the load but it is not the minimum requirement. (NEC 220.12 and Table 220.12)

46. The correct answer is **c**. The purpose of maintaining a minimum distance from the edge of a framing member is to insure that drywall fasteners are not allowed to penetrate the cable. Typical lengths of drywall screws are $1\frac{1}{8}$" to $1\frac{5}{8}$"; therefore, $1\frac{1}{4}$ in. is sufficient in keeping the cable out of harm's way. Choice **a** is incorrect because $\frac{3}{4}$" could place the cable in harm's way. Choice **b** is incorrect because 1" could place the cable in harm's way. Choice **d** is incorrect because maintaining 2 inches from the edge of the bored hole to the framing member would insure protection for the cable. However, this distance would be impractical to maintain as many framing members are not wide enough to support this width on both sides. (NEC 300.4(A)(1))

47. The correct answer is **b**. A thermal protector is a protective device for assembly as an integral part of a motor or motor-compressor that, when properly applied, protects the motor against dangerous overheating due to overload and failure to start. Choice **a** is incorrect because a circuit breaker is a device intended to provide limited overcurrent protection for specific applications and utilization equipment. This limited protection is insufficient to thermally protect motors which are sensitive to excessive heat. Choice **c** is incorrect because a motor circuit switch is a switch rated in horsepower that is capable of interrupting the maximum operating overload current of a motor of the same horsepower rating as the switch at the rated voltage. Choice **d** is incorrect because a surge-protective device is a protective device for limiting transient voltages by diverting or limiting surge current. (NEC 100)

48. The correct answer is **b**. 14 ft. is the maximum distance between supports for a $1\frac{1}{2}$ in. rigid metal conduit. Choice **a** is incorrect because 10 ft. is the maximum distance between supports for a $\frac{1}{2}$ in. to $\frac{3}{4}$ in. rigid metal conduit. Choice **c** is incorrect because 16 ft. is the maximum distance between supports for a 2 in. to $2\frac{1}{2}$ in. rigid metal conduit. Choice **d** is incorrect because 20 ft. is the maximum distance between supports for 3 in. and larger rigid metal conduits. (NEC Table 344.30(B)(2))

49. The correct answer is **c**. Where a metal lampholder is attached to a flexible cord, the inlet shall be equipped with an insulating bushing that, if threaded, is not smaller than a $\frac{3}{8}$ in. pipe size. Choices **a**, **b**, and **d** are incorrect. (NEC 410.62(A))

50. The correct answer is **d**. Section 426.50(A) provides the provisions for the disconnecting means for fixed outdoor snow-melting equipment. Choice **a** is incorrect because Part III of Article 422 provides the provisions for the disconnecting means for appliances. Choice **b** is incorrect because Section 517.17(C) provides the provisions for the disconnecting means for portable equipment. Choice **c** is incorrect because Section 427.55 provides the provisions for the disconnecting means for fixed electric heating equipment for pipelines and vessels. (NEC 426.50(A))

51. The correct answer is **a**. Copper has less resistance than aluminum and therefore will carry more current for an equal sized conductor. Choice **b** is incorrect because aluminum has more resistance than copper and therefore will carry less current for an equal sized conductor. Choice **c** and **d** are incorrect because aluminum has more resistance than copper and therefore will carry less current for an equal sized conductor. (NEC 310 Ampacity Tables, Chapter 9 Table 8)

52. The correct answer is **d**. Poor connections at terminals, a circuit that is too long, and a conductor that is too small for the load can all be a cause of excessive voltage drop. Choice **a** is incorrect because poor connections at terminals can be a cause of excessive voltage drop, but so can the other factors listed. Choice **b** is incorrect because a circuit that is too long can be a cause of excessive voltage drop, but so can the other factors listed. Choice **c** is incorrect because a conductor that is too small for the load can be a cause of excessive voltage drop, but so can the other factors listed. (NEC 210.19, *Informational Note No. 4*)

53. The correct answer is **c**. Choice **a** is incorrect because although you must calculate the ampacity considering both the continuous and noncontinuous loads, you must also consider adjustment and correction factors if they exist. Choice **b** is incorrect because although you must calculate the ampacity considering adjustment and correction factors, you must also consider continuous and noncontinuous loads. Choice **d** is incorrect because once the larger of the two values has been applied, the other factors can be ignored. (NEC 215.2(A)(1))

54. The correct answer is **b**. 125/250V is not considered a nominal system voltage. Choice **a** is incorrect because 120V is considered a nominal system voltage. Choice **c** is incorrect because 208Y/120V is considered a nominal system voltage. Choice **d** is incorrect because 480Y/277V is considered a nominal system voltage. (NEC 220.5(A))

55. The correct answer is **d.** Chapters 5, 6, and 7 may supplement or modify the requirements in Chapters 1 through 7. Choice **a** is incorrect because Chapter 5 may supplement or modify the requirements in Chapters 1 through 7, but so may Chapters 6 and 7. Choice **b** is incorrect because Chapter 6 may supplement or modify the requirements in Chapters 1 through 7, but so may Chapters 5 and 7. Choice **c** is incorrect because Chapter 7 may supplement or modify the requirements in Chapters 1 through 7, but so may Chapters 5 and 6. (NEC 90.3)

56. The correct answer is **a.** In a marina, electrical connections shall be located at least 12 in. above the deck of a floating pier. Choice **b** is incorrect because electrical connections located 24 in. above the deck of a floating pier would be NEC compliant. However, 12 in. is the minimum requirement. Choice **c** is incorrect because electrical connections located 36 in. above the deck of a floating pier would be NEC compliant. However, 12 in. is the minimum requirement. Choice **d** is incorrect because electrical connections located 60 in. above the deck of a floating pier would be NEC compliant. However, 12 in. is the minimum requirement. (NEC 555.9)

57. The correct answer is **a.** Due to possible overheating, the ampacity of each conductor shall be reduced by 70%. Choice **b** is incorrect because a reduction of 80% is applied to conductors where 4–6 occupy the same raceway. Choices **c** and **d** are incorrect because according to Section 210.19(A), a reduction of 80% for continuous load would not be required because the reduction of 70% is larger. (NEC Table 310.15(B)(3)(a))

58. The correct answer is **c.** Table 400.5(A)(1) contains the allowable ampacities for flexible cords and cables. Choice **a** is incorrect because Table 310.15(B)(16) contains the allowable ampacities of not more than three current-carrying, insulated conductors installed in a raceway or cable. Choice **b** is incorrect because Table 400.4 contains specifications for various types of flexible cords and cables. Choice **d** is incorrect because Table 400.5(A)(2) contains the allowable ampacities of cable types SC, SCE, SCT, PPE, G, G-GC, and W. (NEC Table 400.5(A)(1))

59. The correct answer is **a.** The short-circuit rating is not required to be marked on the controller when the short-circuit current rating of the controller is marked elsewhere on the assembly. Choice **b** is incorrect because the short-circuit rating is required to be marked on a motor controller rated for a 480V, 3 hp motor. Choice **c** is incorrect because the short-circuit rating is required to be marked on a motor controller rated for a 480V, 3 hp motor. Choice **d** is incorrect because the short-circuit rating is not required to be marked on the controller when the short-circuit current rating of the controller is marked elsewhere on the assembly. (NEC 430.8, *Exception No. 2*)

60. The correct answer is **d**. The interlocked-type metal-clad cable is more flexible than either smooth sheath or shielded conductor type. Therefore, the allowable bending radius is seven times the external diameter of the sheath. Choice **a** is incorrect because a bending radius of four times the external diameter of the sheath for interlocked-type metal-clad cable would not be NEC compliant, and would likely damage the cable and/or conductors inside. Choice **b** is incorrect because a bending radius of five times the external diameter of the sheath for interlocked-type metal-clad cable would not be NEC compliant, and would likely damage the cable and/or conductors inside. Choice **d** is incorrect because a bending radius of nine times the external diameter of the sheath for interlocked-type metal-clad cable would be NEC compliant. However, it is not the minimum bending radius, which is seven times the external diameter. (NEC 330.24(B))

61. The correct answer is **b**. An overload is a condition caused by operation of equipment in excess of normal, full-load. Choice **a** is incorrect because an ungrounded conductor unintentionally coming into contact with a grounded conductor results in a condition called a short circuit. Choice **c** is incorrect because unintentionally coming into contact with a grounded surface results in a condition called a ground-fault. Choice **d** is incorrect because an overload is a condition caused by operation of equipment in excess of normal, full-load. (NEC 100)

62. The correct answer is **b**. Where angle pull is made, the distance between each raceway entry inside the box or conduit body and the opposite wall of the box or conduit body shall not be less than six times the trade size of the largest raceway. Therefore, 2" × 6" equals a minimum size junction box of 12" × 12". Choice A is incorrect because a 10" × 10" box is too small. Where angle pull is made, the distance between each raceway entry inside the box or conduit body and the opposite wall of the box or conduit body shall not be less than six times the trade size of the largest raceway. Therefore, 2" × 6" equals a minimum size junction box of 12" × 12". Choice **c** is incorrect because a 14" × 14" box meets the NEC requirements, but it is not the smallest allowed. Choice **d** is incorrect because a 12" × 10" box is too small. (NEC 314.28(A)(2))

63. The correct answer is **d**. Grounding electrode conductors shall be bonded to the grounding electrode by means of listed pressure connectors or exothermic welding. Choice **a** is incorrect because grounding electrode conductors shall be bonded to the grounding electrode by means of listed pressure connectors, but this is not the only approved means provided. Choice **b** is incorrect because grounding electrode conductors shall be bonded to the grounding electrode by means of exothermic welding, but this is not the only approved means provided. Choice **c** is incorrect because grounding electrode conductors shall not be bonded to the grounding electrode by means of soldering. (NEC 250.8(A)(1)&(4))

64. The correct answer is **c**. Conductors, not specifically permitted elsewhere in the NEC to be covered or bare, shall be insulated. Choice **a** is incorrect because conductors are supported by the raceway or cable in which they are installed, and this has nothing to do with whether they are covered or bare. Choice **b** is incorrect because conductors, and all equipment and materials, shall be listed as required elsewhere in the NEC. This has nothing to do with whether they are covered or bare. Choice **d** is incorrect because the word *permitted* in this sentence makes no logical sense. (NEC 310.106(D))

65. The correct answer is **b**. Nonmetallic-sheathed cable shall be supported within 12 in. of a metal box. Choice **a** is incorrect because supporting a nonmetallic-sheathed cable within 8 in. of a metal box meets the requirements of the NEC. However, it is not the maximum distance for which the cable may be supported. Choice **c** is incorrect because supporting a nonmetallic-sheathed cable within 4 ft. of a metal box does not meet the requirements of the NEC. Choice **d** is incorrect because supporting a nonmetallic-sheathed cable within $4\frac{1}{2}$ ft. of a metal box does not meet the requirements of the NEC. (NEC 334.30)

66. The correct answer is **b**. Thermal insulation shall not be installed within 3 in. of a non-type IC rated recessed luminaire. Choice **a** is incorrect because space must be provided for heat dissipation around a non-type IC rated recessed luminaire. Allowing only $\frac{1}{2}$ in. of space between the thermal insulation and the luminaire would be in violation of the NEC, and could create a dangerous condition. Choice **c** is incorrect because allowing 5 in. of space between the thermal insulation and the luminaire would be in compliance with the NEC, but it would be impractical for insulating the dwelling from the cold. Choice **d** is incorrect because allowing 6 in. of space between the thermal insulation and the luminaire would be in compliance with the NEC. However, it would be impractical for insulating the dwelling from the cold. (NEC 410.116(B))

67. The correct answer is **a**. Flexible metallic tubing shall not be used in lengths over 6 ft. Choice **b** is incorrect because flexible metallic tubing is permitted and used in dry locations. Choice **c** is incorrect because flexible metallic tubing shall be permitted in accessible locations. Choice **d** is incorrect because flexible metallic tubing shall be permitted where concealed. (NEC 360.12(6))

68. The correct answer is **d**. Intrinsically safe apparatus, associated apparatus, and other equipment shall be installed in accordance with the control drawings. Choice **a** is incorrect because the authority having jurisdiction does not specify how equipment is installed. Choice **b** is incorrect because the insurance company does not specify how equipment is installed. Choice **c** is incorrect because architects do not specify how equipment is installed. (NEC 504.10(A))

69. The correct answer is **c**. Equipotential bonding shall be installed to reduce voltage gradients in the pool area. Choice **a** is incorrect because in equipotential bonding, all metal parts of the pool are bonded together but there is no requirement for a connection to the equipment grounding conductor or system. Therefore, there would be no path for ground-fault current to take. Protection from ground-faults is provided by other means. Choice **b** is incorrect because this bonding would play no role in the operation of the over-current protection device. Choice **d** is incorrect because equipotential bonding shall be installed to reduce voltage gradients in the pool area. (NEC 680.26(A))

70. The correct answer is **c**. An 8 AWG grounded conductor shall be identified by a continuous white outer finish. Choice **a** is incorrect because grounded conductors sizes 4 AWG and larger shall be identified by a distinctive white marking at its terminations. Choice **b** is incorrect because the grounded conductor is a current carrying conductor and must not be un-insulated. Choice **d** is incorrect because the color green is reserved for grounding conductors. (NEC 200.6(A)(1))

71. The correct answer is **b**. All panelboards, other than in dwelling units, shall be provided with electric arc flash warnings if they are likely to require examination, adjustment, servicing, or maintenance while energized. Choice **a** is incorrect because all panelboards, other than in dwelling units, shall be provided with electric arc flash warnings if they are likely to require examination, adjustment, servicing, or maintenance while energized. Choice **c** is incorrect because all industrial control centers shall be provided with electric arc flash warnings if they are likely to require examination, adjustment, servicing, or maintenance while energized. Choice **d** is incorrect because all meter socket enclosures, other than in dwelling units, shall be provided with electric arc flash warnings if they are likely to require examination, adjustment, servicing, or maintenance while energized. (NEC 110.16(A))

72. The correct answer is **c**. A 125-volt, 15-amp receptacle is installed outdoors to provide dedicated power for electric snow-melting equipment, and is not required to have GFCI protection. Choice **a** is incorrect because a 125-volt, 15-amp receptacle is installed outdoors to provide dedicated power for electric snow-melting equipment, and is not required to have GFCI protection. Choice **b** is incorrect because a 125-volt, 15-amp receptacle is installed outdoors to provide dedicated power for electric snow-melting equipment, and is not required to be readily accessible. Choice **d** is incorrect because a 125-volt, 15-amp receptacle is installed outdoors to provide dedicated power for electric snow-melting equipment, and is not required to have AFCI protection. (NEC 210.8(A) *Exception to (3)*)

73. The correct answer is **b**. Receptacles shall be installed such that no point along the floor line is more than 6 ft. from an outlet. Choice **a** is incorrect because receptacles shall be installed such that no point along the floor line is more than 4 ft. from an outlet, to be compliant with the NEC. However, the maximum distance is 6 ft. Choices **c** and **d** are incorrect because receptacles shall be installed such that no point along the floor line is more than 6 ft. from an outlet. (NEC 210.71(B)(1))

74. The correct answer is **a**. A main bonding jumper or system bonding jumper shall be a wire, bus, or screw. A connector is not listed as suitable in Section 250.28(A). Choices **b**, **c**, and **d** are incorrect because a main bonding jumper or system bonding jumper shall be a wire, bus, or screw. (NEC 250.28(A))

75. The correct answer is **c**. The objective is to keep energized feeders at a safe distance from unsuspecting persons who may come in contact with them. 36 inches is considered out of the reach of most people if reaching out a window, door, or similar location. Choice **a** is incorrect because 18 inches is within the reach of most people if reaching out a window, door, or similar location. Choice **b** is incorrect because 24 inches is within the reach of most people if reaching out a window, door, or similar location. Choice **d** is incorrect because 48 inches is out of the reach of most people if reaching out a window, door, or similar location. However, this is not the minimum distance provided by the NEC. (NEC 225.19(D)(1))

76. The correct answer is **d**. Disconnecting means are likely to require examination, adjustment, servicing, or maintenance while energized, and shall have adequate working space for personnel. An access opening of 22" × 22" would be large enough for most workers to safely access the equipment. Choice **a** is incorrect because an access opening of 18" × 18" would not be large enough for most workers to safely access the equipment. Choice **b** is incorrect because an access opening of 20" × 20" would not be large enough for most workers to safely access the equipment. Choice **c** is incorrect because an access opening of 22" × 30" would be large enough for most workers to safely access the equipment. However, it is not the minimum opening size. (NEC 110.26(A)(4)(a))

77. The correct answer is **c**. The maximum voltage for a PV system DC circuits on or in one- and two-family dwellings shall be 600 volts. Choices **a**, **b**, and **d** are incorrect because the maximum voltage for a PV system DC circuits on or in one- and two-family dwellings shall be 600 volts. (NEC 690.7)

78. The correct answer is **d**. A device is a unit of an electrical system that carries current or controls electric energy as its principal function. Choice **a** is incorrect because utilization equipment is defined as equipment that utilizes electric energy for electronic, electromechanical, chemical, heating, lighting, or similar purposes. Choice **b** is incorrect because a circuit breaker is defined as a device designed to open and close a circuit by nonautomatic means and to open the circuit automatically on a predetermined overcurrent without damage to itself when properly applied within its rating. Choice **c** is incorrect because a switch, by definition, is just one example of a device because it controls electrical energy. (NEC 100)

79. The correct answer is **b**. The ability of one coil of wire to induce a voltage into another coil is called mutual induction. This is the principle that supports the operation of transformers. Choice **a** is incorrect because Watt's Law states the relationship between power, voltage, and current. Choice **c** is incorrect because Kirchhoff's Law is a set of laws dealing with voltage and current. Choice **d** is incorrect because Thevenin's theorem is used to reduce a circuit to a single voltage source and a series resistor. (Theory)

80. The correct answer is **a**. Unused openings for circuit breakers and switches shall be closed using identified closures, or other approved means that provide protection substantially equivalent to the wall of the enclosure. Choice **b** is incorrect because receptacles are generally not removed, leaving dangerous holes that create exposure to live electrical components. Choices **c** and **d** are incorrect because unused openings for circuit breakers and switches shall be closed using identified closures, or other approved means that provide protection substantially equivalent to the wall of the enclosure. (NEC 408.7)

Questions answered correctly _____

Questions answered incorrectly _____

Passing score = minimum of 70%, or 56+ questions correctly.

ADDITIONAL ONLINE PRACTICE

Using the codes below, you'll be able to log in and access additional online practice materials!

Your free online practice access codes are:
FVE06XFT3UX623OL478R
FVEDM64PUI11F6736FV5

Follow these simple steps to redeem your codes:
- Go to **www.learningexpresshub.com/affiliate** and have your access codes handy.

If you're a new user:
- Click the **New user? Register here** button and complete the registration form to create your account and access your products.
- Be sure to enter your unique access code only once. If you have multiple access codes, you can enter them all—just use a comma to separate each code.
- The next time you visit, simply click the **Returning user? Sign in** button and enter your username and password.
- Do not re-enter previously redeemed access codes. Any products you previously accessed are saved in the **My Account** section on the site. Entering a previously redeemed access code will result in an error message.

If you're a returning user:
- Click the **Returning user? Sign in** button, enter your username and password, and click **Sign In**.
- You will automatically be brought to the **My Account** page to access your products.
- Do not re-enter previously redeemed access codes. Any products you previously accessed are saved in the **My Account** section on the site. Entering a previously redeemed access code will result in an error message.

If you're a returning user with a new access code:
- Click the **Returning user? Sign in** button, enter your username, password, and new access code, and click **Sign In**.
- If you have multiple access codes, you can enter them all—just use a comma to separate each code.
- Do not re-enter previously redeemed access codes. Any products you previously accessed are saved in the **My Account** section on the site. Entering a previously redeemed access code will result in an error message.

If you have any questions, please contact Customer Support at Support@ebsco.com. All inquiries will be responded to within a 24-hour period during our normal business hours: 9:00 A.M.–5:00 P.M. Eastern time. Thank you!